Blossoms on the Roof

Rebecca Martin

Ridgeway Publishing
Stoneboro, PA 16153

BLOSSOMS ON THE ROOF

Copyright © 2012 Ridgeway Publishing

All rights reserved.

*To order additional copies,
please visit your local
bookstore or contact*

**Ridgeway Publishing
2080 McComb Rd.
Stoneboro, PA 16153
USA
ph: (888) 822-7894
fax: (724) 376-2090**

Illustrated by Laura Yoder

ISBN: 978-09848888-5-6

Printed in the United States of America

Table of Contents

The Big Blue Umbrella 5
Paddy Long 11
Abraham's Obedience 19
Happy Hearts 27
Free Land 35
Eskimos and Huskies 43
Train Ride 51
Kettie and Mattie 61
Home at Last 69
A Roof Made of Grass 77
A New Team 83
Firewood and the Indians 89
Picnic with the Oxen 95
Firebreak 101
Fire! 107
Good Bye, King 113
The Secret 121
Rain at Last 127
Cold 133
A Feeling in the Air 141
Long Night 147
Promised Blessings 153

Author's Note:

The people in this story are imaginary, but many of the things really happened. In 1894 some Amish families moved to North Dakota. Sod houses, prairie fires, blizzards, and droughts were all part of pioneer life in North Dakota.

Amish Frontier Series

Blossoms on the Roof

The Treasure Hunt

A Song for the King

Paradise Valley

Arrow in the Sky

Steamboat Rock

Chapter 1

The Big Blue Umbrella

Polly stood with her nose pressed to the windowpane. "The rain has stopped. Can we go to Grandma's now, Mom?" she begged.

Mother came and stood beside her, studying the clouds that tumbled away to the horizon. "It does look as if the rain is over—for now. But the weather seems unsettled. What if another shower comes up? You need to be back by supper time, because it's Saturday night."

Ten-year-old Ben had a solution to that problem. "Grandma has that blue umbrella, you know. I'm sure it's big enough for Polly and me to walk underneath. Don't you think so, Polly?"

"Oh, yes. Grandpa opened it up one day, and it was huge," replied Polly.

Ben's eyes danced. How many times had he stared longingly at that shiny, blue umbrella hanging behind Grandpa's front door? How many times had he imagined what fun it would be to walk in the rain while holding up a roof to keep dry? He certainly hoped it would start to rain when it was time for him and Polly to come home.

Mother was still looking out the window. "All right, you may go. I do want Grandma to get this note today." Carefully she folded the paper on which she had written a letter for her mother-in-law. "Polly, you may put this in your pocket."

"I want to go, too!" begged four-year-old Jakie when he saw Ben putting on his hat. Jakie was so excited that his red hair bounced up and down.

Mother said firmly, "No, Jakie, today you can't go to Grandpas. It might rain again soon, and you mustn't get wet. Remember, you still have a cough."

"I'm all well again," Jakie pouted.

"No, you are not all well, even if the cough is better," Mother said, just as firmly. "Now Ben and Polly, you had better be off if you want to be back in time for supper."

Grandpa and Grandma Yoder lived a half mile down the road. Half a mile is not far to go for an eight-year-old girl and her ten-year-old brother. Certainly not when new, dark clouds are boiling up from the western horizon!

"It could start raining any minute," said Polly.

Ben eyed the clouds. "Let's run."

And run they did, while the cold March wind nipped

at their heels and the clouds rolled across the sky.

"I'm—I'm not even cold," Polly puffed when they reached Grandma's porch.

Ben laughed. "I'm hot! Running keeps you warm." He reached up to knock at Grandma's green-painted door.

Polly grabbed his arm. "It's my turn to knock. Remember, you did last time."

"Okay." He let his arm drop.

Knock, knock. Polly gave the door two good, hard raps.

Just like that, the door popped open and Grandma's round, wrinkled face beamed out at them. "Come in, come in!" she invited them.

Polly knew exactly where to hang her bonnet in Grandma's kitchen, and Ben knew exactly where to hang his hat. Beside the door were four wooden pegs. Polly and Ben knew the story behind those pegs. Grandpa had put up those pegs at just the right height for a girl to hang her clothes.

"Here's a note from Mother," Polly announced, fishing for the folded paper in her pocket.

"Thank you," said Grandma. "I must get my glasses." Perching her gold-rimmed spectacles on her nose, she read Mother's note carefully.

Polly hoped Grandma would tell them what the note was about. But she did not.

Well, she did mention one part of it. "Your mother writes that you may stay for twenty minutes, then you must hurry home again. She also writes that if there is anything you can help me with, I'm to set you to work."

Grandma smiled at Polly and Ben. "You know, I could

use someone to sweep the porch. And someone to churn the butter." Grandma was a very busy person, because two grown sons still lived at home to help with the farm, yet both her daughters were married.

"I'll churn the butter," Ben offered quickly.

"And I'll do the porch." Polly grabbed the broom and went to work.

Up and down, up and down went the plunger of the big wooden butter churn. Ben listened carefully to the glug-glug sound inside. Ben knew the cream had turned to butter, when the glug-glug turns to a splashing noise.

Polly had just swept the last corner of the porch when Ben shouted, "It's butter now! I can hear it."

"Good," said Grandma. She opened the churn, poured off the thick, white buttermilk, then fished out golden globs of butter. "Here, I will put some butter into a jar for you to take home."

"Oh, thank you," said Polly. "We don't have butter very often since we sold our cow."

Grandma's kitchen was silent. All three of them knew why the Yoders had to sell their cow. Polly wished she hadn't mentioned it.

"And here are cookies for you because you were my good helpers," Grandma said briskly. "I'm afraid your twenty minutes are up already."

"Thank you," said Ben, munching on the cookie. Then he looked out the window and said happily, "Oh, it's raining again."

Grandma was puzzled. "Why are you so happy about that?"

Ben's eyes slid to the blue umbrella hanging near the door. He knew he shouldn't ask to use it. But ever since Grandpa had bought it last year, Ben had longed for an excuse to use it.

Grandma saw him glancing at the umbrella. "You could use our umbrella to walk home in the rain," she suggested.

A big grin lit up Ben's face. Another grin lit up Polly's face. Ben promised, "We'll take very good care of it."

"Come out here on the porch and I'll show you how it works," Grandma said.

Ben laughed. "I know why we have to go out on the porch. If we opened that umbrella in here, we could never get it through the door!"

"See this little white button?" said Grandma. "First you push it—like this." Click. Just like that, the umbrella blossomed into a big, round roof!

"Now push it way up, past that other little button—so. The umbrella is locked in place now." And with that, Grandma put the smooth, black-and-gold handle into Ben's hands.

He beamed. "See, Polly? There's lots of room for two under here." Down the steps he went, out from under the porch roof. Rain began drumming on the fabric of the umbrella—but not a drop landed on Ben. "This is great, Grandma," he said. "I've never held an umbrella before."

"Wait," called Grandma. "I have to warn you about one thing. Always keep the umbrella turned towards the wind. Do you understand?"

"Yes," said Ben, although this was only partly true. He

understood that the round dome of the umbrella must always face the oncoming wind. But he did not understand why.

Clutching the gift of butter, Polly joined him under the umbrella. They waved good-bye to Grandma and set off.

Chapter 2

Paddy Lang

"While we are on Grandpa's driveway, I must keep the umbrella turned this way," Ben planned. "Then when we go out on the road, I must turn it. 'Always face the wind'. That's what Grandma said."

Polly trotted happily alongside her brother, watching the rain streaming off the edges of the umbrella and splashing down into the puddles.

After a while Ben said, "I think I know what would happen if we turned the umbrella so that the wind could get beneath it."

"Oh?" said Polly. "What would happen?"

"Why, it would be like sailing a ship," Ben crowed. "You know that picture of a sailing ship Grandpa keeps in his desk?"

Polly nodded. "You mean the ship on which his grandpa sailed to America."

"Right. In 1809." Ben and Polly had heard the story of their ancestors so often that they could not forget the date. More than eighty years had passed since Grandpa's grandpa had left his home in Europe to come to America.

"Anyway," Ben went on, "a sailing ship works because the wind blows into the sails. So if I let the wind blow into my umbrella—"

"You'd fly away!" cried Polly, her eyes round.

Ben laughed so hard that he almost lost his grip on the umbrella's handle. "So you think I would go sailing away, over Grandpa's field, and even over the roof of his barn? No, it wouldn't be like that; all I'd have to do is run very fast to keep up with the umbrella. Wouldn't that be fun?" He glanced up and down the road to make sure there were no buggies coming.

"Don't do it," begged Polly. " I couldn't keep up. Then I'd get wet. And besides, Ben. . . "she placed a hand on his arm. "It would be wrong. Grandma told us not to, and you promised."

Ben shook off her hand. Polly was a good sister, but sometimes he wished she weren't quite so good. He wished she had more adventure in her bones.

That was what Grandpa had said one day about Father: "He's got adventure in his bones." Ben wanted to be like Father, always ready to try something new. But he couldn't if Polly was around.

"You won't do it, Ben, will you?" Polly implored again.

"Aw, no, I guess not," he replied. "We're almost home anyway. Careful, I have to make a quarter turn with the umbrella now as we turn into our lane."

Now the umbrella was to their left; when they started off at Grandpas', it had been to their right. "The wind stays the same," Polly said, "but we have to change directions."

Then it happened. Ben peered out from beneath the umbrella, and what he saw excited him so much that he forgot to keep it turned toward the wind. Poof! The wind gusted beneath the umbrella. How it tugged!

Ben managed to hang on. But he did not sail away over the fields and rooftops. With a sickening crack, the umbrella turned inside out!

Polly wrung her hands. "It's ruined! Why did you do it?"

"I didn't do it," Ben shot back. "At least, not on purpose. It just happened." Sadly he inspected the remains of the umbrella. The gleaming spines were crumpled pieces of wire now. The fabric looked like a tattered, burst balloon.

Polly wailed. "Oh, why did you forget?" Neither of them thought about the rain, even though they were getting wet.

Ben pointed toward the hitching-post in front of their white clap-board house. "Why did I forget? Because I saw that."

Polly let out a little gasp. "Oh, it's him again." Tied to the post was a brown horse hitched to a topbuggy that everyone knew very well. It was painted green, and the folding top was bright yellow.

Suddenly, the wind grabbed the umbrella.

No one else in the district had a buggy like that. If you saw it in your yard, you knew that Paddy Lang had come to pay a visit. And if you were renting one of Paddy's farms, then you were not glad to see him. Not in this year of 1894, the second year of a depression that had left millions of people without jobs and without money.

"Many people," Mother kept reminding the children, "are without food too. But by the grace of God, we live on a farm, so we can raise our own food."

The last time she'd said that, Father had put in, "Providing we can buy seeds. We can't raise food without seeds."

Mother had reminded him, "We can plant all those potatoes we couldn't sell last year."

"But what if nobody has money to buy potatoes this year?" Father had asked.

"Why, we'll eat them," Mother had replied. To Ben, that hadn't seemed like a real answer to the very real problem of how to buy seeds. Looking at Paddy Lang's brightly-painted buggy, he guessed Father was in the house talking with Paddy. And Ben knew what they were talking about. The rent. The money the Yoders owed Paddy for this farm.

Polly said worriedly, "The last time Paddy came, we sold the cow to pay the rent. I wonder what we're going to sell this time?"

"Well, I just hope we never have to sell Jasper and Rob." Ben looked over to the pasture, where their team of dapple-gray horses stood near the gate. The rain had stopped; the late-afternoon sun sent slanting rays across the field, touching the horses' white manes with gold.

"And I hope we don't sell Flip either," said Polly, stooping to pat the black and white puppy who came bounding to meet them.

"Huh. Nobody would give any money for Flip," snorted Ben. His eyes turned to the ruined umbrella again. To think that he had almost planned to disobey Grandma! How terrible that would have been, if the umbrella had been destroyed because of his disobedience. Having it happen by accident was bad enough.

He set the umbrella down near the front steps. "No use taking it inside if Paddy Lang's here," he said to his sister.

"I don't even want to go in. I don't like the way he talks to Mother and Father," Polly said unhappily.

Ben paused with one foot on the bottom step. "Well, I guess we could go to the barn."

Polly shrugged. "I don't like going to the barn either."

Ben knew why she said that. These days, the barn was just too empty. First they had sold two calves. Then they had sold the ten sheep. Then—worst of all—they had sold Lilac, the cow.

Before Ben and Polly could decide where they wanted to go, the door opened and Paddy Lang stepped out.

Mother had once said that Paddy's last name should be Long, not Lang. He certainly was a long man. Over six feet tall, he had long legs, long arms, a long face and a long nose. Even his hair was long. His gray locks bounced on the collar of his green-black coat as he walked.

Paddy looked at the children with piercing black eyes. "Where have you been?"

"Uh—at Grandpas," Ben stammered.

"Oh. Well, good-bye." He walked out to his shiny buggy, untied the horse, and drove away.

Polly ran into the kitchen. "Oh, Mother, was he mean?" She looked from Mother's face to Father's face.

Mother sat in the rocking chair, holding baby Lisbet. "No, Polly, Paddy wasn't mean. He has never been mean."

"But he—he made us sell all our animals!" Polly burst out.

"No, he did not, Polly," Father said kindly. "We ourselves decided to sell our things because we needed to pay our rent if we wanted to keep on living on Paddy's farm. We owed it to him. We want to be honest."

Now Ben had a question. "But why does he make us pay the rent when he knows we can't make any money with his farm these days?"

Father turned to look at him. "Well, you might say that Paddy Lang is a good businessman. And today he was very good to us. We offered to sell the team—"

Ben held his breath. Not Jasper and Rob!

". . . in order to pay the rent," Father went on. "But Paddy said no, we couldn't farm without the team. So he will give us more time."

"Shall I get the dishes, Mother?" Polly asked. There was no supper on the table, yet it was supper time.

"Yes, please. The soup is ready."

Polly didn't need to ask what kind of soup it was. Potato-and-turnip soup, of course, because those were the only two vegetables they had left in their root cellar. As long as they had onions and cabbage and carrots, Mother had made other kinds of soup. But this spring it was always potatoes and turnips, sometimes with a few lumps of dried beef or salt pork added.

"Father, I ruined Grandpa's umbrella," Ben said unhappily. "I happened to turn the wrong way, and the wind caught it."

"Oh, that's too bad," said Father, getting to his feet. "Where is the umbrella?"

Ben led him out to the front steps. "I never knew an umbrella could turn inside out."

"I guess you had no reason to know much about umbrellas," Father said kindly. "As far as I know, Grandpa is the only one in church who owns an umbrella."

He took the poor, crumpled thing in his hands and turned it over several times. "I think we might be able to fix this."

"Really?" Ben said hopefully.

"Yes. I will use a pair of pliers to straighten these spines. I will pull the fabric back in place and mend this tear. It won't be as good as new, but it will work."

Polly came to the door in time to hear that. "Oh, I'm so glad you can make it right again. And Mother says to come in. Supper's ready."

Chapter 3

Abraham's Obedience

On Sunday morning, Mrs. Mouse woke up Polly. Mrs. Mouse lived in a cranny beneath the rafters of Polly's loft room. (You see, the rafters were the ceiling, and they sloped right down to the floor. The only place you could stand up straight in Polly's room was in the middle, where the roof peaked.)

Polly lay on her straw mattress for a few minutes, listening to Mrs. Mouse at work. Scratch-scritch-scratch. Polly wasn't sure what mice worked at, but they always seemed to be doing something. And they made a lot of noise doing it, too, considering how small they were.

Dawn was just creeping in through the one tiny

window under the gable. Perhaps if she lay still for a while longer, Polly thought, there would be enough light to see Mrs. Mouse when she skittered out of her hole.

Sure enough, there she was—a soft gray form hurtling along the inside of the eaves. Where was she going in such a hurry, anyway? Did she have a family hidden away somewhere?

Maybe she had six children. Polly began thinking up names for six tiny balls of gray fur: Fuzzball, Sooty, Softy. . .

"Polly! Ben! It's time to wake up. We're walking to church this morning, you know." Mother's voice cut urgently into Polly's list of names.

Polly popped out of bed. Mouse names could wait for another morning. Today was Sunday, the best day of the week, when all the families of the west district would meet at Abram Millers for church.

Brrr, it was chilly here under the rafters. But this early-March chilliness wasn't nearly as cold as the icy draughts that had seeped through the cracks of the loft in January and February. In minutes, Polly had buttoned her homespun dress.

Between the two loft rooms was a tiny hall with a trapdoor. Polly pulled it open, thinking smugly that she'd been quicker than Ben this morning. All winter they had been trying to see who could be first down the ladder in the morning.

Even before she touched the bottom rung, Ben's feet appeared above her. She had to scramble to get out of the way!

"I wasn't far behind you," he huffed, grabbing his hat and coat. Though the Yoders' chores had dwindled to almost nothing, Ben still went out before breakfast. He liked to be the one to bring Jasper and Rob their oats, out by the gate.

Mother stood near the cast-iron cookstove, stirring the porridge. Last night she had set the crushed wheat kernels to soak in water, and this morning as soon as the fire was going, she had them bubbling in the pot. Sometimes on Sunday mornings when breakfast had to be early, the wheat porridge tended to be quite crunchy because there was hardly time to boil it enough.

Hearing a whimper from baby Lisbet's cradle, Polly hurried over and picked her up. Lisbet was seven months old. Her round, pink face was adorable, with that round button nose, round red mouth, and round brown eyes.

Oh, there was Father, coming in with the water pail he'd filled at the well. Polly had hoped it would be at least a few minutes longer till breakfast. She did not like crunchy porridge.

But there was Ben too, his cheeks red from the morning air. "Pretty cold out there," he said as he washed his hands at the basin. "Good thing we're walking today. We'd get cold feet if we rode in the wagon."

Mother brought a sleepy-eyed Jakie from his trundle bed in the bedroom. They all sat down at the smooth board table Father had made for Mother when they got married. Touching the table's satiny surface, Mother had once said to Polly, "Father spent a whole week scrubbing and rubbing to get this top so smooth."

They bowed their heads to give thanks. Then Mother passed the porridge, and Polly ladled some, steaming hot, into her bowl. Next came the sorghum pitcher. She liked to pour the sweet, brown syrup in a criss-cross pattern over the top of her porridge.

Ben poked her elbow. "Hurry up. We haven't got all morning. It's nearly two miles to Abram Millers."

Quickly she handed him the pitcher. He dumped his sorghum in one big splash and passed the pitcher on to Father.

Yum. In spite of the crunchiness, the porridge was delicious. Eating something hot helped chase the shivers on a windy morning like this.

Half an hour later the Yoder family started off. Father was carrying Lisbet for now, but Polly knew what would happen after a quarter mile or so. Jakie would start complaining that he was tired, and Father would hand the baby to Mother or Ben so he could pick up the four-year-old in his strong arms.

"I'm glad we can take the bush road this morning," Polly said to Mother. "The trees keep the cold wind away."

"That's right," said Mother. She peered up into the tops of the tall oak and beech trees. "It won't be long now till we'll see little green buds coming out on the trees."

"Maybe we can even plant our fields soon," Ben said eagerly. Then his face fell as he added, "If we can get seeds."

Nobody said anything. Nobody liked the thought of leaving fields bare just because there was no money for seeds.

At the next crossroads, two families joined the Yoders. Soon the bare fields were forgotten and everyone was talking and laughing again. Polly liked walking with her friend, Susan Mast. On school mornings, it was the other way around: Susan came walking along and Polly joined her.

By the time they neared Abram Millers, four families were walking together on the narrow dirt road. Suddenly Ben called, "Get off the road. Aaron Gingerich is coming with his team."

Everybody strung out in single file near the ditch to let Aarons' prancing black team pass. Aarons had five miles to the Millers, and that was why they hitched up this morning even though most of the other families walked. Aarons' Lena and Anna waved from the wagon as they passed by.

Soon everyone was sitting on backless benches in Abram Miller's house. It was a tight fit to get all the families in, but fortunately Abrams had a bigger house than the Yoders. When church was at Polly's home, the people usually sat in the Yoder's barn loft.

"Oh Gott Vater, wir loben Dich," the congregation sang. Ben helped sing as best he could. He did not understand all the German words of the song, but Father had once told him that it was a hymn of praise.

Soon Henry stood up to preach. Henry had dark brown hair and dark eyes that shone like black coals. "Sometimes when I am splitting wood for our cook stove," Henry said, "I think of Abraham. Do you know why? Because the Bible says that Abraham was splitting wood one morning. Was his heart heavy? I don't know. It could have been, because God had asked him to do the hardest thing: sacrifice his only son.

"Abraham didn't hesitate. He got up early in the morning. I like to read about that morning, and the preparations Abraham made. He saddled his ass. He hired two of his servants to go along. And he split the wood for the offering.

"Then there was only one thing left to do: Go. And go they did—for three days. For three whole days, Abraham and Isaac and the servants walked, not knowing to which mountain God was taking them. Then at last, we read that 'Abraham lifted up his eyes and saw the place from afar off.'

"Now Abraham and Isaac went on without the servants. We can hardly blame Isaac for being curious. He asked his father, 'I have the wood—you have the fire and the knife—but where is the offering?'

"Abraham's reply was mysterious. 'God shall provide Himself a lamb.' Dear young people, I challenge you to put yourself in Isaac's place at this moment. Isaac could have asked more questions. He could have demanded a more solid answer. But he was satisfied, and he obeyed.

"Oh, what a picture of obedience is this story of Abraham and Isaac! Abraham obeyed God, Isaac obeyed his father. We do not read that the lad struggled when Abraham placed him on the wood he had split for their offering.

"And how greatly they were rewarded for their obedience. Not only was Isaac's life spared, but God also promised great blessings. God told him, 'In thy seed shall all the nations of the earth be blessed; because thou hast obeyed my voice.'

"And that," said preacher Henry to wind up his story, "is a blessing that reaches down to us today. Because those words are actually a promise of the coming of Jesus Christ, the greatest blessing the world has ever seen."

Chapter 4

Happy Hearts

"What is a blessing?" Polly asked on Monday morning at the breakfast table.

"So you heard when the minister spoke of all the blessings God gave to Abraham?" Father asked.

Polly nodded. She could not speak because her mouth was too full of sorghum-sweetened porridge.

"When God blesses us," said Father, "it means He is protecting us and making us happy."

Ben said thoughtfully, "Then I guess He isn't blessing us these days."

Father looked at him. Mother looked at him. "Why do you say that?" they both asked at the same time.

"Well, we're having all these troubles. No money to pay rent and buy seeds . . ." His voice trailed off.

"When I said God makes us happy, I didn't mean that He gives us everything we like," Father explained earnestly. "I meant that He gives us happy hearts, in spite of the troubles that come along."

"Oh-h-h-h," Ben said slowly.

"I like to think of Uncle Ben," Father went on. "Maybe that's why we named you after my brother. Because, even though life has dealt him some hard knocks, he has a happy heart."

In his mind's eye, Ben pictured his uncle, who looked so much like Father with his dark hair and beard. Uncle Ben's back was so crippled that he needed a cane to walk. But yes, Uncle Ben's brown eyes usually shone with cheer when they visited his cobbler shop.

"Yesterday," Father recalled thoughtfully, "Preacher Henry said that God gave Abraham many blessings. Do you remember why God blessed Abraham?"

"Because he obeyed," Ben said.

"Right. Abraham believed and obeyed God. Today, faith and obedience are still the key to God's blessings," Father declared.

Mother got up from her chair. "Polly, we had better comb your hair."

Polly hurried to the little mirror above the basin and opened her braids. Just like Jakie's, her locks were a reddish color. Polly wished she could have shiny gold hair like Ben. And like Mother. Nobody else she knew had red hair—except Jakie.

Father had put on his hat. "I am going away this afternoon," he announced. "I want to talk with some men over in La Grange County. Since I'll be riding Jasper, it will take me at least four hours to get there. I'll be staying overnight, and I won't come back till tomorrow afternoon."

Ben blinked. "You'll be gone for twenty-four hours?"

"That's right." Father smiled. "Hurry home from school so Mother won't be lonely."

Ben waited for Father to explain why he needed to talk with these men in La Grange. But Father just put on his coat and went outdoors. "Is it a secret?" Ben asked Mother.

"You mean the reason for his trip?" Mother paused. "Well, I think he'd rather explain when he gets home." She smiled at Ben. "Remember what we heard about Isaac yesterday? He was satisfied with Abraham's answer even though he didn't understand."

Ben looked down at his boots. He didn't like secrets. He would feel better once he knew why Father needed to go on such a long trip.

"Let's go," chirped Polly, grabbing the tin lard pail that contained their lunch—good brown bread with apple butter and salt pork, and one slice each of Mother's delicious crumb pie.

"I wonder," said Ben as they marched out the lane together, "I wonder if Father's trip has anything to do with Paddy Lang's visit on Saturday?"

"How could that be?" asked Polly.

"Well, maybe he will find a way to make some money to pay the rent," came Ben's answer.

Polly frowned. "How do people 'make' money,

anyway?"

Ben laughed, "You thought Father would go and manufacture some coins? No, no, I meant that he might find work to earn money."

"Oh," said Polly, feeling just a little bit hurt. After all, she was only eight years old and couldn't be expected to understand everything. . . Then she brightened up and exclaimed, "There come Susan and John!"

As always, Ben and John strode on ahead while the girls kept their own leisurely pace down the road. The school was not far away; they were sure to be on time, so why hurry?

Turning a bend in the road, they saw a little schoolhouse at the crossroads, half-hidden by a grove of oak trees. "Oak Grove School" said the sign on the neat split-rail fence. More children were coming from every direction. Happily they milled about the yard until the big brass bell on the roof gave three loud clangs.

In streamed the children—all thirty-eight of them—leaving their wraps and lunches in the cloakroom before entering the classroom. There at the far end behind her scarred, black desk stood Miss Mulligan, looking as stern as ever. (Though she was called Miss, she was old—at least fifty—and had been teaching for many years.)

Miss Mulligan's iron gray hair was drawn back into a prim bun. Her eyes were a strange greenish-brown color. She had a thin nose that twisted to the left, as if it had been broken sometime long ago. She always wore the same style of dress: iron-gray wool, the color of her hair.

Promptly and efficiently the classes began. Miss

Mulligan was strict, yes, but the children liked school. They liked the steady, dependable routine. They liked their teacher's crisp, no-nonsense ways.

Polly was so absorbed with her lessons that she forgot Father's trip. But Ben thought about it often. In fact, right after lunch when he was supposed to be studying history, he grew a little sleepy and began half-dreaming. It seemed to him that he saw Father plodding along toward La Grange on a donkey. On the donkey's back was a pack of split wood...

Bang! Miss Mulligan's ruler came down on Ben's desk. "You are not studying your lesson," her sharp voice rapped out.

Ben jumped. The picture of Father and the donkey disappeared. Obediently he bowed his head to read the history book again.

"You looked so funny," Polly giggled, later that day when they were almost at home. "Why, you jumped this high! Were you sleeping?"

"Naw," Ben said grumpily. He didn't like it when Polly laughed at him. "Just daydreaming, I guess. I wonder where Father is right now. I wonder whether he has reached La Grange."

"Oh, I'd forgotten about Father going away," Polly confessed.

Ben was surprised. "You'd forgotten? I kept thinking about him all day."

Jakie came running to them across the yard, his short legs churning as fast as they could go. After him galloped the black and white puppy. Jakie yelled, "Father is gone.

Father's gone for the night."

Though only ten, Ben was big for his age. He picked up Jakie the way Father often did, twirling Jakie's feet off the ground. "We knew that," he said. "Father told us this morning that he's going away."

"And he's coming home tomorrow," Jakie went on. He put his arms around Ben's neck. "Do you know what we're having for supper?"

"No. Tell us," begged Polly. Her mouth watered already at the thought of a special treat.

"Pancakes!" declared Jakie. "With real fresh butter. Grandpa brought some butter today."

Polly dashed up the porch steps. She could hardly wait for those pancakes.

Mother smiled at the children. With a wooden spoon, she was stirring something in a blue china bowl. "Guess what! The chickens laid three eggs today. Spring is coming!"

"Ah, that's why we can have pancakes," Ben said wisely. He knew that pancakes needed eggs. He also knew that the chickens stopped laying eggs in cold weather, but in the spring when they could get outdoors and eat more good things, they started laying again.

Watching Mother drizzling the butter into the pan reminded Ben of something. Grandpas had been here today; they had brought the butter. "Mother, did you give the umbrella back to Grandpas?" he asked.

"Yes, I did."

"I wish it hadn't been ruined," Ben mourned.

"They were sorry to see what happened," Mother told

him. "But they knew it was an accident, and they were glad to see Father repaired it."

Soon the first pancakes were sizzling in the pan. What a good supper that was! The golden-brown pancakes were crisp at the edges and soft as a feather pillow in the middle. "Too bad Father isn't here to help us eat these," Polly remarked.

Ben's mouth was too full of pancake and sticky-sweet syrup to say anything. But he nodded his head vigorously up and down in agreement. Not having Father at the table was the only bad thing about this supper.

Chapter 5

Free Land

The next afternoon when they came home from school, there he was on the porch, waiting for them. "Father!" screamed Polly, running to meet him.

Ben ran too, and soon Father had an arm around each of them. "You were gone so long," Polly whispered.

"It's good to be back," said Father. "Now come in and I will show you something."

On the table lay a big piece of paper. "A map!" exclaimed Ben, bending for a closer look. "Here's where we live." He put his finger on the state of Indiana.

"The railroad company gave me this map," Father said, pointing to the big letters at the top that said GREAT

NORTHERN RAILWAY. "Do you see this railway running west and north from Chicago?" His finger followed a line that looked like a twisting ladder. On and on went his finger, across the states of Illinois, Wisconsin, and Minnesota.

Then his finger stopped, on a square shaped state. "This is North Dakota, where the United States government is giving away free farm land." He paused, looking at Ben and Polly. "And we are going up there to get a home of our own."

"What?" said Ben. He looked from Father's face to Mother's face. They were both smiling.

"Yes," said Father, "we are moving to North Dakota. That's why I went to La Grange County. Some families from there are starting off this month, and we plan to join them."

"North Dakota," said Ben slowly, trying to get used to the idea. He studied the map again. "Why, that's almost up in Canada!"

Father nodded. "Right on the border."

"It must be awfully cold in North Dakota," Ben said. "Some people in Canada live in houses made of snow."

"You must mean the Eskimos," Father said with a chuckle. "They live much farther north than the border. Canada is a huge country."

"How far away is North Dakota?" Polly asked in a small voice.

"It's more than six hundred miles, to the area where the other families have claimed homesteads," Father replied. He pulled another paper from his pocket. "Now this shows you the area where we will live—Rolette County. Here's the railroad, going up to the town of Rollo. Here's Island Lake. We plan to get a homestead in Island Lake township."

"Will we be near the lake?" Ben asked eagerly.

"Maybe. I won't know till we get to the land office exactly where our farm will be," answered Father.

Ben was full of questions. "How big will the farm be?"

"We will be getting 160 acres of free land. Well, almost free. We must pay $16 to the land office in order to stake the claim."

"Imagine!" marveled Ben. "One hundred and sixty acres. We can grow bushels and bushels of grain."

"Not in the first year," Father said.

"Will we have to cut down a lot of trees, the way Grandpa's Father did when he came to Indiana?" Ben wondered, recalling Grandpa's pioneering stories.

This brought another chuckle from Father. "There are no trees in this part of North Dakota. It's prairie! Acres and acres of flat land, no stones, no trees."

"Then why can't we plant crops this spring?" Ben wanted to know.

"Because the prairie is covered with tough, high grass. We will plow as much as we can, to plant a garden and maybe some flax. But it won't be much the first year," he said again.

Ben said soberly, "Plowing prairie grass will be hard work for Jasper and Rob."

"Yes," said Father. "I learned that many farmers use four-horse teams. Or oxen."

"Will there be a log house on our farm?" wondered Polly.

Father looked at her. "There will be no house at all, Polly. We will need to build one. That is another reason why we cannot plant many crops this spring."

"A sod house, Polly. We are going to build a sod house," Mother told her.

Polly's eyes were round and questioning. "What is a sod house?"

"Why, we plow up the prairie grass to make strips of sod about five inches thick, and we pile up the strips like bricks to make the walls," Father explained.

Polly blinked. "The house will be made of dirt?"

"Earth and grass and roots, all together in a nice solid strip," said Father. "I'm told that sod houses are quite warm in the winter."

"But," said Ben, "what will we burn in our stove if there are no trees?"

Father's finger came down on the map of North Dakota again. "Do you see this funny-shaped area? That is a mountainous area where there are lots of trees. It's called the Turtle Mountain Reserve, because that's where the Indians moved to when the white men began settling the land."

"Indians!" exclaimed Polly, her eyes growing wider still.

Father patted her hand. "Friendly natives, Polly. Anyway, what I wanted to say is that we can fetch all the wood we want in those hills. Wood for burning and wood for building."

"You said the house will be of sod," Ben reminded him.

"Yes, but we'll use wood sooner or later." Father folded up the maps. "I think Mother wants to put supper on the table."

Ben had more questions. "Have those other men seen the land already?"

"Yes. They traveled out there last spring, and saw many acres of wheat fields. Lord willing, some day there will be wheat fields on our farm, too. The United States is growing so fast, there is a great demand for wheat. We can make money growing wheat," Father said with a dreamy note in his voice.

"And out in North Dakota, there'll be no Paddy Lang coming to see us about the rent," Ben said happily.

Mother brought the plates and cups. "We'll be like Abraham—going to a land we haven't seen."

"We need to be like Abraham," Father said earnestly. "We need to have faith in God and obey Him, too."

Between mouthfuls of potato-and-turnip soup, Ben had more questions. "Will we go by train, Father?"

"Yes, we will," said Father, smiling when he saw how the children's faces lighted up.

Polly clapped her hands. "Oh, good! I've never had a train ride, but Jakie has. Remember, Jakie, when you went with Father and Mother on the train to Pennsylvania to visit our other Grandpas?"

Jakie put down his spoon and wrinkled his forehead. "Train?" he repeated, trying to remember.

"To think you had a train ride but don't know it anymore," Polly said sadly. "Well, you were only one year old. Just a baby, actually."

"Now we're going on a train again?" Jakie asked. All this talk about North Dakota and train rides was more than his four-year-old mind could grasp.

"Yes. You know how a train looks. We've seen one coming into town," Ben told him. "That big, smoking engine on the track, with dozens of cars coming along behind. And we'll be in one of those cars!"

"Car? Ride in a car?" Jakie queried.

"Oh, now you're all mixed up," Polly laughed. Jakie had sometimes seen an automobile too, and he knew those "horseless carriages" were called cars. She explained. "The railway cars are like—like houses on wheels, being pulled along by the big engine."

Ben turned to Father. "What about Jasper and Rob? How will they get to North Dakota?"

"There will be several cars especially for livestock," Father answered. "You see, on this train that is leaving Goshen on March 28, there will be many, many families who are moving to North Dakota—not just the five Amish families we know of. So there will be cars for passengers, cars for freight, and cars for livestock."

"So we can take our cookstove, and this table, and—and our beds?" Polly wanted to know. Her eyes circled the room, spotting so many things she would hate to leave behind.

"We can take all the furniture that's necessary," replied Father.

Ben was puzzled. "But Father, where will we get the money for the train fare?"

Father's eyes glistened, as if a few unshed tears lurked there. "Both our Grandpas will loan us money. And so will Uncle Ben."

"Oh," said young Ben. He pictured his uncle, toiling away in that dingy little cobbler shop, mending people's harnesses and shoes. He was pretty sure that Uncle Ben did not have a lot of extra money. Yet he was willing to help Father with this pioneering venture. Suddenly Ben understood why there were tears in Father's eyes.

Chapter 6

Eskimos and Huskies

"I can hardly wait to tell Susan," Polly panted. She had to run to keep up with Ben as they went out the lane the next morning.

"And I wonder what John will say. He'll probably wish he could go, too," Ben planned. "There he comes around the bend now." Off Ben sprinted to meet his friend.

"Susan—we—we are going to North Dakota!" puffed Polly as soon as she reached the other girl.

Susan stopped short and stared at Polly. "What? You are going on a trip. I thought you said there's no money to pay the rent."

"No, no," laughed Polly. "We are not going on a trip.

Well, yes, we are, but then we'll stay there. In North Dakota. Where we can get a free farm from the government."

Susan started walking slowly, scuffing her feet in the mud. "Oh. You are moving away. But not soon, I hope?"

Her voice sounded so sad that Polly hardly knew what to say. "Well, yes. At the end of this month."

"Oh, Polly. I'll never see you again." Two big tears shone in Susan's blue eyes.

Suddenly Polly felt like crying too. Up to now she had only thought of the exciting parts. Moving to North Dakota had sounded like a marvelous adventure. But this was different. Now she started to think of all the friends she would leave behind. Was it true? Would she never see them again?

In a very small voice she said, "Maybe we'll come back to visit. With the train, you know."

"Oh," Susan said again, just as forlornly as before. "How far away is North Dakota?"

"More than 600 miles," Polly's voice was almost a whisper.

"Six-hundred-miles." Susan pronounced the words with a long pause between each one, as if to let them sink in. "Why, that's like the other side of the world, Polly."

Polly swallowed hard. Was that a sob, trying to push up into her throat? But she must be brave. "No, it's not, Susan. Father showed us on the map. North Dakota is in the United States, so it can't be on the other side of the world."

"Oh." It seemed Susan had run out of things to say.

Meanwhile, Ben and John were also talking about North Dakota. John's first comment was, "Why, that's almost up in Canada, where the Eskimos are."

"No, they—" Ben started to say.

But John interrupted. "My Father heard that some Amish are moving up there, but I never dreamed it would be anyone I know. Guess what Father said about North Dakota, Ben: the winters get so cold that the smoke from your stove freezes before it ever leaves the chimney."

Ben stared at his friend. "That's not true. Smoke can't freeze."

"Well, Father said so," John replied with a shrug. He pushed open the school gate and shouted to the other boys, "Guess what! Ben's going to move up to Eskimoland!"

Ben was stunned. He had not dreamed that John would react like this. Stopping inside the gate, he waited unhappily to see how the other boys would respond.

They crowded closer to John, casting curious glances in Ben's direction. "What did you say? The Yoders are moving?" questioned Tom Ghent, the curly-haired son of an Irishman.

"Yep," John answered importantly. "Up to North Dakota. You know, that cold place where they're starting an Amish settlement."

Harry Pontocki guffawed, "Oh, yeah. Where it gets so cold nights that your breath freezes on the blankets and you have to break the ice before you can get up in the morning."

Ben stood miserably nearby. This was so different than

he had imagined. He had pictured himself in the center of the crowd, holding everyone's attention as he told about the planned move. Instead, John was telling the others, and the only kind of attention he was getting was scorn.

Ed Dupont yelled over to Ben, "You'll have to kill a polar bear and make yourselves fur coats to keep warm."

And Adam Rheal piped up, "Might as well trade in your team for a bunch of husky-dogs to pull your sled."

Ben had never been so glad to hear the clang of the big brass bell. He scurried in ahead of the other boys and was in his seat before anybody else could think up a scornful remark.

The desks were double ones, two students on each bench. Ben wasn't sure if he imagined it, or was his seat mate Billy Teddinton edging as far away as possible on the bench?

With so much misery inside him, Ben found it hard to focus on his lessons. He glanced over in Polly's direction. She didn't look very happy, either. Had the girls treated her badly, too? How could their schoolmates be so mean?

Lunch hour was no better. As often happened, they planned to play "Wolf-dog", a game invented by an earlier generation of Oak Grove students. On each side of the schoolhouse they drew a "wolf-cage" in the mud; in each of the four cages a student was stationed, to be a "wolf". Each "wolf" owned ten twigs which he called his "bones". The rest of the children were "dogs" whose object was to steal as many "bones" as possible without being tagged by a "wolf", who could never set foot outside his cage.

Today the game took a strange new twist. "Let's call the

wolves "huskies", suggested Tom, and the rest agreed with cries of delight.

That was bad enough. Ben knew why they were doing it. But the worst part was when the "huskies started chanting, "Look out, here comes an Eskimo," whenever Ben or Polly drew near to steal bones. Then the "husky" would growl fiercely and make faces at them.

"Pretend it doesn't bother you," Ben whispered to Polly when he brushed past her. But he could see in her eyes that it did bother her a great deal.

It was the longest lunch hour Ben had ever experienced. How glad he was to return to the classroom, even if Billy Teddinton slid to the far side of the bench again.

Ben took one look at Miss Mulligan, standing straight and stern at the front of the classroom, and his heart dropped. What now? Her eyes flashed the way they usually did when there was trouble ahead.

"Your talk of Eskimos and husky dogs," she snapped, hands on hips, "is absolute nonsense."

Ben swiveled his eyes, trying to catch glimpses of his classmates without turning his head. (When Miss Mulligan was speaking in that tone, you just froze. You didn't dare move.)

Out of the corner of his eye he could see that the others were dumbfounded. Really, they shouldn't have been surprised that Miss Mulligan had heard about the Eskimos. Everyone knew she had eyes in the back of her head, and ears front, back, and sides.

"North Dakota," she continued—and her voice could

have frozen smoke in the chimney—"is situated just below the 49th parallel, which is the the border between the United States and Canada. Many different crops and vegetables are grown in North Dakota. It has millions of acres of prime farm land, just being opened to settlers." Her voice softened. "And if I were younger, I would be boarding a train for North Dakota, too."

At that moment, Polly wanted to run up, grab her hand, and plead, "Yes, do come with us. We want you for our teacher." Of course she didn't say it but she gave Miss Mulligan one of her best smiles.

"Now," said Miss Mulligan, "let's get on with our lessons."

She never said it, but everyone understood: not another word was to be said about Eskimos in connection with North Dakota.

Like magic, the other boys' attitudes had changed when school let out. Now they asked Ben friendly, interested questions about North Dakota and the train ride. Now too, Ben thought he could detect a trace of envy in some of the boys.

"After all," he said to Polly when they were almost at home, "just staying here in Indiana looks pretty tame when you have a chance to go pioneering."

Polly nodded. At least Ben was happy again. But in the evening when they were washing dishes, Polly said to Mother, "That was the worst day I've ever had."

Mother looked at her. "Are your friends sad that you're leaving?"

"Uh—well—Susan is. But some of the girls made fun

of—of North Dakota. And called us Eskimos." She had not cried all day, but now a sob pushed up into her throat.

Mother put an arm around her shoulders. "I'm sorry, Polly. I hadn't thought they would do that."

Sniff—"neither did I"—sniff. Polly wiped her nose. "But it was better after Miss Mulligan gave us a tongue-lashing." She wasn't even sure what a tongue-lashing was, but she'd heard the other girls using the word.

"Miss Mulligan has no use for nonsense, does she?" Mother asked gently.

"No. She called the talk about Eskimos absolute nonsense." Polly giggled. "And she said she'd like to go to North Dakota, too."

"Good for her," said Mother. She looked Polly in the eyes. "I hope you didn't make a fuss when the others were giving you a hard time. The Bible says of Jesus that "when He was reviled, reviled not again". That means He didn't talk back when people mocked Him and scorned Him."

"I tried not to make a fuss," Polly whispered. And it was true. Even though she had wanted to scream at her classmates that they were being unfair.

Chapter 7

Train Ride

Packing was fun. Mother started on the last Saturday morning before they were to leave, so Ben and Polly could help. Into Mother's high-top, wooden trunk with the polished brass hinges, they carefully placed the dishes. Towels and bedding were just the thing to pack around the plates and the teapot and the blue china bowl, to keep them safe on the long trip.

Father got some scrap lumber at the lumber yard in town and nailed together six boxes. All the other household things, and many of Father's tools, went into these boxes. Of course, they had to keep out a few things to use over Sunday, because they would not be leaving until next week.

"I guess the table and chairs don't need to be packed in boxes," Ben remarked, caressing the smooth table-top. "They can just go in the wagon, then we'll pile them in the freight car."

Father came into the house just then. "I'm sorry," he said slowly. "We've decided we can't take the table and chairs."

"O-h-h-h-h," wailed Polly. "But you made them yourself." He had made the chairs too, out of yellow pine lumber that shone warmly at night when the lamp was lit.

"Isn't there room in the freight car?" Ben asked.

Father sat down on one of the chairs. "Oh, yes, there would be room. It's because of the rent. You see, we still owe Paddy Lang rent for this farm. We want to do what's honest and pay that rent. Paddy said he will accept the table and chairs for payment."

"O-h-h," said Polly again. This time it was not a wail, just a sigh. She had thought they were finished with Paddy Lang. But now, after taking the sheep, the cow, and the calves as rent, he would take one more thing: their beautiful table and chairs.

"Someday," Father promised," I will build a new table and chairs."

Ben wondered, "What will we use in the meantime?"

"These packing-boxes may have to do for a while," Father answered. "But as soon as we have a house, I will cut some trees in the Turtle mountains and build a make-shift table."

Polly asked, "What is a make-shift table?"

"When something is make-shift, it is roughly built and

meant only to be used until we have something better," Father explained with a smile. "When we have made enough money selling our wheat crops, I can buy lumber to make a table just as good as this one."

Ben said gloomily, "We can't even plant wheat this year."

"It's true that we will be suffering hardships for a while," Father said thoughtfully. "Let's look at it this way: hardships will help remind us that we are only strangers and pilgrims on this earth. One day we hope to be with the Lord in a better place."

The kitchen was very quiet. Even Jakie looked sober, as he tried to understand what Father meant.

Polly wasn't sure she understood. But she did notice when the minister said almost the same thing the next day in church. He was talking about Abraham again. He said that Abraham lived only in tents. He did not live in big houses, because he had faith in God and was seeking a better country. "Heaven is the better country that we all seek," the minister said.

Sunday was a happy-sad day for Polly. She was happy to see all her friends again. Yet she was sad because she might not see them for a long time after this.

Monday was next. On Monday, when Polly came home from school, she hardly knew what to do. Their things were all packed. All she could think of was Tuesday, when they would have to get up early and drive to the train station with Jasper and Rob.

Tuesday was the end. The end of life in Indiana. Grandpa and Grandma came over, even though it was so early in the morning. They said they would rather say good-bye here than at the train station. They hugged and kissed everyone, then it was time to go.

Polly sat on the tail of the wagon. She waved and waved to Grandpa and Grandma, standing there in the yard of their old home. She waved until her arm grew tired, and then the wagon went around the corner and she could not see their old home anymore.

What a surprise waited for her at the train station! There on the platform, in front of a big crowd of people, stood Susan.

"Oh, Mother, I have to go to her," Polly begged as she climbed from the wagon.

Mother looked at all the people milling about. "You must stay near me. You would get lost if you wandered around by yourself. Besides, I need you to watch Jakie and Lisbet while I help Father and Ben load our things into the freight and livestock cars."

The freight cars had been parked here last week. Yesterday, Father had brought one load of their things, and today they had brought the rest in the wagon with them.

"I will watch Jakie and Lisbet," Polly promised obediently. "Maybe Susan and her father will come over here."

She was right. In a few minutes, Susan was at her side. She explained, "I begged Father to bring me. John is here too. They want to help load your things. We won't get to school till nearly noon, but that doesn't matter."

"Maybe Miss Mulligan won't mind," Polly said. "After all, she said she would like to climb on a train to go to

North Dakota."

"Today I feel like doing it too. I feel like I want to go with you," admitted Susan.

Already they could hear the train whistle, far down the line. Puffs of black smoke appeared above the trees. Then the big red and black engine came steaming around the bend, going slower and slower.

It took awhile for the engine to shunt on the siding and hook up the freight cars. Susan and Polly stayed close to Mother, Jakie and Lisbet. Polly felt a little frightened about the many strangers milling about. To think that they all wanted to go to North Dakota too! She hoped it was a big place, so everyone would have room.

Everything was loaded. Father and Ben came back, saying that Jasper, Rob, and Flip were safely in the livestock car along with the other horses and some cows.

It was time to board the train! Susan gave Polly one last hug, then she stepped back. Father gripped Polly's hand tightly, picked up Jakie, and led the way to the passenger car.

They sat on wooden seats just inside the door. What a big coach it was! Dozens of people filled the rows of seats. Up above the seats were strange, wide shelves. Father explained that those were bunks where they could sleep at night.

Clouds of smoke and steam began drifting past the window. Ben whispered excitedly, "The engine is getting up steam!"

Soon Polly felt the car jerk—once, twice, again—then they were moving forward. Faster and faster they went,

It was time to board the train!

while the wheels clackety-clacked beneath them, and the coach swayed from side to side.

"Like a ship," grinned Ben. "We could imagine we're on a ship, like Great-Great Grandpa when he came over from Europe. It feels almost like we're riding waves."

Father said across the back of the seat, "I think ocean waves are often a lot rougher than this."

At first Polly kept busy staring out the sooty window. Farms and fields and villages fled by at a tremendous speed. But soon the car's rocking motion made her feel sleepy. She had been up early this morning. Before she knew it, she was fast asleep with her head down on the arm rest.

When she awoke, the train had stopped. How bewildered she felt! Rubbing her eyes, she stared at the soot-stained windows. "Is it morning?" she asked.

Ben laughed, "You are all mixed up. It's not morning—it's late afternoon, and soon it will get dark."

Polly felt like crying. Everything was so strange. She could hardly see through the window. What were those tall, square shapes she saw out there? Were they in North Dakota already? She didn't dare ask, for fear her brother would laugh again.

Mother noticed Polly's bewilderment. She reached across the back of the seat to pat her shoulder. "We are in Chicago, Polly. That's a big city with many, many buildings."

Now she knew what the tall shapes were. Noticing that Father's seat was empty, she asked, "Where's Father?"

"He went to help feed and water the livestock. That's

quite a chore. When he gets back, we'll eat supper. Then soon it will be bedtime."

Bedtime. Suddenly there was a funny, hollow feeling in Polly's tummy. She wished she could just climb the ladder to her little bedroom in the loft at home.

Ben was wishing nothing of the kind. "It's going to be fun, Polly! You and I get to sleep in those bunks up above. Father and Mother will just pull back their seats and sleep down here. Lisbet and Jakie will lie on blankets on the floor."

Polly eyed the bunk above her head. "What if I fall out?" she asked in a trembly voice.

"You won't," Mother was quick to assure her. "There's a sturdy railing. The rocking of the train will help you fall asleep tonight, just as it did this afternoon."

Ben said excitedly, "Here comes Father now. I'm hungry for supper." The big basket of food Mother had brought was on the floor near his feet. As soon as Father had taken his seat, the family gave thanks. Then Ben handed out the thick slabs of brown bread to each one.

While they ate, fresh clouds of steam and smoke puffed by the window. The train was starting again. Faster and faster they rocked along past the buildings of Chicago.

"What a big city this is," Polly whispered in awe. "When will we come to the end?"

"I don't know," Ben said, crunching on a slice of raw turnip. "See, the lights are coming on in the buildings now."

Polly clapped her hands softly. "How pretty that looks!" She was sorry when they had passed the last building. She would never forget the sight of so many lighted windows, twinkling like stars in the night sky.

Pressing her nose against the window, she stared out into the velvety darkness. "When will we see another light? Doesn't anybody live here? This must be a desert."

"No, it's not," Father chuckled. "Maybe all the people on the farms hereabouts have gone to bed already."

"Oh, there's a light now," exclaimed Polly. "It's moving. Maybe it's a mother carrying a pail of fresh milk and a lantern." Dreamily she thought how that used to be, walking in from the barn with Mother after she had milked the cow. In North Dakota they would have a cow again, and a barn, and fresh milk every day. . .

"Bedtime, Polly." Father's voice cut into her dreamy thoughts. "We will pray now, then we'll show you how to climb into the bunk."

The climbing was the worst part. Once settled on the thin mattress, Polly was quite comfortable. The sheets smelled of soot. So did the curtain which hid her from everybody else. She was shut away in a private little world of her own. But down below were the comforting sounds of Father and Mother putting Jakie and Lisbet to sleep.

Chapter 8

Kettie and Mattie

"Wake up, Polly," Father said through the floor of her bunk. "We're in Wisconsin now."

"Wisconsin?" Polly rubbed her eyes. What a strange feeling, to wake up in a different state from the one she'd gone to sleep in!

Polly parted the curtains and peered around the car. Cheerful morning light filtered through the sooty windows. All around her, in the bunks and on the seats, people were waking up. Some were eating breakfast from their hampers.

Right across the aisle from the Yoders was a family with two little girls. Yesterday Polly had kept glancing at the girls, and they had kept glancing back. Several times they had smiled at one another. Now Polly watched as the two girls clambered down from their bunk and shrilly asked their mother what they would have for breakfast.

Suddenly hungry, Polly climbed down too and asked the same question. Father smiled. "In fifteen minutes or so, the train will stop. I'll check the livestock and see if our chickens have laid any eggs. How would you like fresh eggs for breakfast?"

Polly made a face. "How would we cook them?"

Mother pointed to the far end of the car. "Haven't you noticed that stove? See, somebody is frying eggs now. We will wait till it's our turn, then I will take a pan and cook some eggs for us."

"I'm hungry," whined Jakie.

"Here, you may have some bread for now," Mother offered. "It might be a while before we can cook our eggs."

Just then the train jerked to a stop. Polly looked out the window and saw a dingy station and a few buildings. "This isn't a very big town," she said.

Father and Ben hurried out. When they came back, they brought a surprise. "How about some fresh milk for breakfast?" Father asked, holding up a jar. "Another farmer was milking his cow. He said it's more milk than he and his family can drink today. So he's sharing it with others."

"Mmm," Polly said, taking a long swallow of the rich milk. "And what about Flip? Is he happy there in the livestock car?"

Ben chuckled. "Flip had to learn to get along with two other dogs. They're doing fine now, though there was some snapping and snarling at first."

"I hope the other dogs don't hurt Flip," Polly fretted.

"Don't worry, Flip can take care of himself," Ben said.

Mother went off to fry the eggs, and when she returned, the Yoder family ate them right out of the pan. You couldn't wash dishes on a train. Yet everyone agreed that it had been a delicious breakfast.

By this time, the train was pounding along the track again. When Polly looked out the window she saw dense forests and high, rocky bluffs. Off to the left, she caught a flash of silver. "Is that a lake?" she wondered.

"No, that's the Mississippi River," Father informed them.

"Really?" exclaimed Ben. He had learned about this vast river at school. "I wish we'd get closer. I want to get a good look."

"At St. Paul we will cross the river," said Father.

Plunk. Something soft landed on Polly's lap. She knew right away what it was. Yesterday she had seen the girls across the aisle playing with two balls. Polly liked the soft feel of the ball in her hand. The ball was homemade, out of pink cloth.

Polly looked across the aisle. There were the two girls, putting their hands to their mouths and giggling. "Is this your ball?" Polly asked, holding it up.

Both girls nodded. They giggled harder.

Polly looked at the ball. Should she throw it back? She decided not to. Sliding right to the edge of the seat, she reached across the aisle.

"Thanks," whispered the bigger of the two girls as she

Polly soon made friends on the train.

took back the ball.

"Did you make the ball?" Polly asked shyly.

The other girl shook her head. "Aunt Lona did. She made us each one. For going away gifts."

"Are you moving too?" Polly wondered.

The girls nodded again. "To North Dakota."

"So are we." Suddenly they seemed like old friends. "I'm Polly."

The girls looked at each other, both waiting for the other to speak first. "I'm Keturah," the older one said. She had wispy brown hair and brown eyes. "Everyone calls me Kettie."

"And I'm Matilda. . . well, Mattie," said the younger, whose hair was the color of shining straw.

"I hope we live near each other in North Dakota," Polly said impulsively.

The other two nodded. "Then we could go to the same school."

For a while it seemed they had run out of things to say. Then Kettie confided, "I'm glad we don't have to go to school until October."

"Why? Don't you like school?" exclaimed Polly. She had been sorry to hear that they would not start school in North Dakota until the fall.

Kettie shrugged. "I'm scared. Everyone will be strange."

"Oh, I see." Polly said slowly. Kettie was right. At that moment she felt homesick for Miss Mulligan, in her iron-gray dress, for Susan, and for all her other friends at the school back in Indiana.

"Well, at least we'll have each other—if we go to the same school," Mattie reminded them.

Much to Ben's delight, the train reached St. Paul before dark. "Let me sit by the window, Polly," he begged. "I want to see the Mississippi."

"But I want to see it too," Polly complained.

"Here. I'll squeeze in beside you," Ben said, shouldering his way to the window.

Polly wailed, "Ow, you're pinching me. I can't even see!"

"Ben, be careful," Mother warned.

He edged over to give Polly more room. "Ooooh, that's a big river. Do you see it now, Polly? Way down below the bridge?"

"Yes, I see it," Polly said, still feeling grumpy because he had shoved her around.

Father told them, "We are in Minnesota now. Soon we will reach the town of Minneapolis, where the train will stop to let us take care of the animals again."

Polly never saw Minneapolis. She was sound asleep before the train stopped, and by the next morning the train was steaming through the forests and fields of Minnesota.

That day, Polly learned to know the Miller girls. They and their mother had come to sit with Polly and her mother while Ben and Father had left their seats. "I hope North Dakota is big enough for all these settlers," said Sarah Miller, who was thirteen.

"If there isn't room for everyone, we'll just go back home again," Lizzie Miller said cheerfully. She was only a little older than Polly. Then there was Mary, who was a year younger than Polly. By the time they went back to their own seats, Polly was hoping the Miller girls would go to her school, too.

In the afternoon, the train came to the Red River. "This is the boundary between Minnesota and North Dakota," Father announced. There was excitement in his voice. "Look at the river, Ben. Do you notice something unusual about the water?"

Ben peered down through the trestles of the bridge. "Why, this river flows northward!"

"Yes," said Father with a smile. "It goes right up to Canada into Hudson Bay."

"Right up to the Eskimos," Ben said in awe.

The train rolled through the town of Fargo and on into the country. Samuel Miller came walking down the aisle and told Father, "Last fall when we were here, we saw thousands of acres of wheat. The Red River valley has some of the most fertile soil in the States!"

Ben asked immediately, "Will our farm be in the Red River valley?"

"No, we are settling farther west," Father replied.

"The soil out in Rolette County, where we are going, is not quite so deep and rich. But it is still good wheat country," Samuel assured them.

Every now and then the train passed through a small town. People stood near the rails, waving and cheering.

"They know this is an immigrant train. They are happy to see more settlers coming," Father said.

"Why?" asked Polly.

"Maybe they are a bit lonely," Mother told her. "North

Dakota is a big, empty land."

"Oh," said Polly soberly. Just the way Mother said it made her feel a little lonely, too.

"Pretty soon this place won't be empty any more," Ben declared. "North Dakota, here we come!"

Chapter 9

Home at Last

Far away on the horizon of that big, empty land, the sun was starting to go down. The train slowed. From across the aisle, Kettie asked excitedly, "Do you see that town? That's where we get off. Father says our farm in only six miles from here."

"Is this our town too, Father?" Polly wondered.

"No. Remember, we are going to a town called Rollo."

Polly looked sadly across the aisle at Kettie and Mattie. They had heard Father's reply. They were sad, too.

Now the train had stopped. Kettie and Mattie helped their parents gather up the baggage. "Goodbye," they said to Polly. "Surely we'll see you again soon."

"Goodbye," Polly replied. She felt like crying. North Dakota was big. What if they never saw each other again?

Ben watched the passengers pouring off of the train. "Will those people all sleep in this little town tonight?"

"No. Some of the passenger cars will be unhooked here. Of course, the freight cars with their belongings will stay here, too," Father answered.

As they left town, the train seemed to move faster than before. Maybe it was because so many cars had been left behind.

Darkness had fallen when the train stopped again. "Here we are," Father said softly. "This is Rollo. Tomorrow, as soon as the sun is up, we will load the wagon and drive to our new home."

"I don't know if I can sleep tonight," Ben said. "I'm too excited." He went out to help Father care for the livestock.

Polly climbed up into her berth. She could not sleep right away. Maybe it was because the train stood still. Tonight she would not be rocked to sleep.

Then suddenly it was morning and she heard Mother say, "Polly, wake up. We are going home this morning, remember?"

Home. Where was home? Back in Indiana, on the farm that belonged to Paddy Lang? No, home was here in North Dakota, somewhere out there on the prairie. Polly climbed down quickly.

Mother told her, "Father and Ben are hitching up the team. They loaded the wagon early this morning. We will eat breakfast on the way." She picked up a sleepy Lisbet, and Polly took Jakie's hand.

"Goodbye, train," Polly whispered as she stepped off the passenger car. For more than two days, this had been her home on wheels. Now it was time to find her home on the prairie.

There were Jasper and Rob, already hitched up, jiggling around as if they could hardly wait to get going. The wagon was piled high. "Is there room for us, too?" Mother asked with a smile.

Father swung Lisbet and Jakie up on the seat. "Mother, you may sit on the seat. Ben and Polly, you can find room in the back."

Polly squeezed in beside one of the packing boxes. Ben sat on top of the box. Father looked back to make sure everyone was ready. Then he lifted the reins, and they were off.

Minutes later, they turned off the street. Now the wagon rolled along in high, waving grass. Swish, swish, swish went the wheels in the grass. Polly peered down beneath the wheels. The road was nothing more than a muddy track in the grass.

"I wonder how Father can find the road," said Ben from his perch on the box. "I can hardly see it."

At first the horses trotted, but after awhile they slowed to a walk. The grass swished against their legs as they plodded along.

"Nothing to be seen but grass," reported Ben from his lookout. "Acres and acres of grass."

"Like an ocean," laughed Polly. "We are on an ocean again. An ocean of grass."

The sun rose higher in the sky. "I see a house and

barn!" called Ben.

Polly stretched her neck. "Where? I don't see a house."

"There. Those humps. The buildings look like grass, because they're made of grass."

"That is a house?" Polly rubbed her eyes, as if she had been dreaming. "Will our house look like that, too?"

"That's what sod houses look like," Father told her. "They are really quite comfortable. They don't look very high, but inside they are dug down. As soon as we get to our place, we will start building our house."

"Oh," said Polly. She watched the small, low, sod house until it disappeared from view in the waving grass. Soon they passed another sod house, then another.

"How will you know which is our farm?" Ben called to Father.

"I will check the number on the stake. Have you noticed those stakes driven into the ground? They mark the corners of the 160-acre plots," Father replied.

At last the horses stopped. Father got down and checked the stake. "This is it!" he declared. "This is our farm."

Polly looked around. All she saw was grass. And more grass.

Ben stood up on the box. "I see some trees. I think there's a creek back there."

"Then we will build our house near the water," Father decided. "Giddap, Jasper and Rob. Just a little bit farther."

They stopped near the trees. Ben was off the wagon in an instant. Polly followed him down to the creek. Patches of gray snow still clung to the north bank. The water looked icy cold.

Cupping his hands, Ben drank some. "Mmm. Fresh water. The water we had on the train wasn't very good anymore."

After drinking some water too, Polly climbed back to the bank to see what Father and Mother were doing. Already, Father was hitching Jasper and Rob to the plow. In town he had bought an attachment meant especially for cutting sod strips.

"Now watch us make bricks out of this sod," Father said to Mother.

The horses strained forward. The plow bit into the grass. Slowly, a strip rolled away from the plow. Ben used a knife to cut the strips into three-foot pieces.

After a while Father had cleared a patch of bare soil. Now the horses could rest while Father and Ben started building the house. They began piling sod strips, like bricks, around the bare patch.

"Will the house be finished by tonight?" asked Polly.

"No," said Father. He grunted as he lifted one of the big sod 'bricks'. "It will take us some days."

Even Mother helped a little to carry and lift the bricks. Soon it was time to get dinner. Mother got some firewood in the wagon. They had brought firewood from Indiana because Father had said there were no big trees on their farm. They would have to fetch their wood far away in the Turtle Mountains.

Mother opened the cookstove lid and put in the wood. Polly laughed and said, "Will you use the cookstove out here in the field?"

"Yes," answered Mother with a smile.

Polly helped peel potatoes for dinner. "My hands are cold," she said. She held her hands over the cookstove.

The spring wind was chilly. The whole family huddled near the stove to eat the good, hot potato soup.

Father declared, "It's a real treat to have soup, after two days on the train."

After dinner, Father and Ben began cutting more bricks. Mother put Lisbet and Jakie to sleep on the south side of the wagon, where the sun helped to keep them warm. Polly felt sleepy, too. Soon she lay down beside Lisbet.

Building a sod house was hard work.

When she awoke, she heard Father saying to Mother, "We should start off soon if we want to go to town for the night."

"Couldn't we sleep here?" Mother suggested. "Some of us could be in the wagon. And the new house wall would be a shelter for the rest of us."

Polly scrambled to her feet and said, "How can we sleep in a house without a roof?"

"We will put up blankets for a makeshift roof," Mother told her.

"Tomorrow, Ben and I must go to the forest to cut poles. A good roof needs poles laid across," said Father.

Polly thought, I'm glad we will have a wooden roof. A house made of grass is all right, but it will be better with a wooden roof.

For supper, the Yoders ate the rest of the potato soup. They had just finished eating when a man, a woman, and two small children came strolling along the track. Ben whispered to Polly, "They must be our neighbors. Look, the man has hair the same color as you and Jakie."

Polly looked again. The newcomer was tall, with a freckled face and sandy hair. Maybe there was a hint of orange. But to Polly, the man's hair did not seem nearly as red as her own.

"Hello," called the man. "I'm Bill McIlelan and this is my wife, Cynthia."

Cynthia was small and pretty, with white-blond hair and blue eyes. She introduced their children, saying their names were Thomas and Aileen.

Bill said in his booming voice, "Since we're neighbors,

we thought we'd come and see if there's anything we can do to help. I see you have started your house."

"Yes. It went quite well. Tomorrow we must make a trip to the forest for roof-poles," Father told him.

"No need for that," Bill exclaimed. "I have a pile of poles at my place that you could use for now. Later you can get some to replace them."

"We'd appreciate that," Father said.

Bill helped Father and Ben with the housebuilding until the sun went down. Cynthia helped Mother and Polly make the beds. They stuffed the mattresses with sweet-smelling grass. On the wagon, they fashioned a blanket-covered spot where Ben and Jakie would sleep.

Inside the new sod walls, they put up two more blankets, almost like tents. In one 'tent' was a mattress for Polly and Lisbet. In the other was one for Father and Mother.

Darkness was falling as Bill and Cynthia left for home. Mother said happily, "We have good neighbors."

Polly shivered in the cold night air. How glad she was to snuggle under her woolen blanket! Just before she fell asleep, she stuck her head out from beneath her 'tent'. There were the stars, hundreds and hundreds of them, like pin-pricks of light in the huge, black, prairie sky.

Chapter 10

A Roof Made of Grass

"Polly, please get some water from the creek!" called Mother, first thing the next morning.

Off went Polly, her skirts swishing in the dew-covered grass. There was Father with Jasper and Rob, already cutting more bricks. He had been up before the sun.

Near the creek, Polly heard a sharp chip-chipping sound. Two bright little black eyes peered at her from a hole in the ground. The animal was brown with white stripes running along its body. With a flick of it's striped tail, it disappeared into the burrow.

Polly ran home as fast as she could with her pail of water. "Mother, I think I saw a chipmunk!" she panted. "It was striped and brown and tiny, no bigger than a kitten."

"Ah," smiled Mother. "You must have seen a flickertail squirrel. Bill told Father that North Dakota has many flickertails."

Polly clapped her hands. "What a nice name! I hope I can make friends with the flickertails. The one I saw looked friendly."

Mother put some wood on the fire in the cookstove. When Father came in for breakfast, she told him, "The firewood we brought along is nearly used up."

"Then we must make a trip to the forest next week," replied Father.

"How can we cook without firewood?" Polly wanted to know.

Mother knew what to do about that problem. "We must find some buffalo chips."

"What's that?"

Ben put in, "Have you forgotten what buffalo are, Polly? Miss Mulligan taught us about them. Thousands of buffalo used to live on the prairies."

"Of course I remember the buffalo pictures she showed us," Polly snapped. "But what are buffalo chips?"

"The chips are dried dung left by the buffalo years ago," Mother explained. "Many pioneers in the west have used chips for cooking."

Polly made a face. Dried dung did not sound like good fuel to her. But when Mother and Jakie set off to hunt for chips, Polly went along, too. Soon their basket filled up with hard, dry chips.

"What if we meet a buffalo?" Polly asked. She remembered how fierce the animals had looked in Miss

Mulligan's book. They had huge, shaggy humps and broad heads with curved horns.

"We won't see a buffalo," Mother smiled. "Even though there were millions of them on the prairies a hundred years ago, almost none are left. They were killed by the buffalo hunters."

In a way, Polly felt sorry about all those buffalo being killed. Still, it was a comfort to know they wouldn't meet one.

They did see four more flickertails. Jakie squealed with delight and tried to catch them, but they were too fast for him.

Flip wanted to catch them too. His paws worked furiously as he dug into a hole where a flickertail had dived down.

"Come on, Flip," called Mother. "You will never dig down to that flickertail's den. They have long burrows."

They moved on down the creek. Mother told Polly, "Flickertails have more than one doorway to their homes. Even if Flip should dig all the way down into the den, the flickertail would be long gone through his back door."

"Flickertails are smart," Polly said admiringly.

A nice surprise waited for them at home. Bill and Cynthia were there, helping to build the walls! Polly played happily with the four little children, the rest of the day.

Before the McIlelans left that night, the men moved the cookstove into the house. Even without a roof, the stove helped to warm the house.

In his bedtime prayer, Father thanked God for their

new home. He asked God to bless their family, and all the other families pioneering on this vast, new prairie land. Then he asked God to bless their friends and relatives in Indiana—especially Grandpa and Grandma.

That made Polly feel a little homesick. How nice it would be to run down the road once again and see Grandma!

On Saturday morning Ben was eager to start putting up the roof. "Maybe we can have the house finished by tonight!" he said.

Father shook his head. "I'm afraid not. Putting up a roof is hard work for one man and one boy. But we can start, anyway."

Then along came a happy surprise. Peter Masts came driving up with their six children in the team and wagon.

"We want to help you build your house," Peter said as he and his boys unhitched the team.

"Is your house finished already?" Father asked.

"Not quite. But we have more help than you do," replied Peter, looking at the three Mast boys who were older than Ben.

Father said happily, "Building our roof will be much easier with so much help."

Polly watched them lifting the poles into place. "Why don't they put the poles closer together?" she asked Mother. "The rain can get in between them."

"They will lay sod bricks on top of the poles," Mother explained.

"Oh." Polly was disappointed. They would have a roof made of grass after all. She had hoped for a wooden roof.

But she did not say that to Mother.

Now Father was cutting some long grass with the scythe. When Polly asked what he needed that for, he said, "We will put a layer of grass across the poles before we put the sod on top."

"Why do we need a layer of grass?" came Polly's next question.

"Think about it, Polly," said Father. "When you are sitting in our new kitchen, which would you rather see above your head—grass or soil?"

"Grass, of course," Polly answered promptly.

"If we didn't put on a layer of grass, you would be looking at the underside of sod bricks," Father pointed out. "Besides making a nicer ceiling, grass will also help keep the rain out."

By evening, the Yoder home was quite snug. Mother hung a blanket over the door and said, "This will do until Father has time to build a door."

Mother also hung curtains to divide the house into rooms. One tiny bedroom was for Ben, one was for Polly, and the third was big enough for Mother, Father, and the two little ones.

The next day was Sunday. "I wish we could go to church," Polly said wistfully. She longed to see Susan and her other friends. She wished she could sit on the familiar, worn benches and listen to Abe or Henry preaching.

"Next Sunday all five North Dakota families will get together," Father promised. "We planned that on the train. Today we will have church just for our family here in our new sod house."

So they sang songs together and Father read from the big leather-covered Bible. He read the story of Jesus blessing the little children. Polly imagined how happy the children must have felt to be near Jesus and to feel His hands touching them.

"The disciples thought Jesus is too busy for children," Father said. "They told the mothers to take the children home again. But Jesus called them back. He wanted to bless the children."

Father put the Bible back in the packing box where it was kept. "Do you remember one of our last Sundays in Indiana, when Henry preached about Abraham and Isaac? God rewarded Abraham's obedience with many blessings. And do you remember what Henry said was the greatest blessing the world has ever known?"

"The coming of Jesus," said Mother.

Father nodded. "So from this story of Jesus and the children, we know His blessings are for the little ones, too." He smiled at Ben, Polly, Jakie and Lisbet.

Polly looked around their little house. It smelled of damp earth and grass. It was gloomy because not much light could get in the window. But Polly knew that Father was right about those blessings.

Chapter 11

A New Team

"Today," announced Father, smiling at Polly and Ben, "you may help Mother plant our garden."

Polly clapped her hands. "May I get the seeds?"

"Yes, you may," answered Father.

Polly left the table and went to the packing box that was their storage cupboard. She knew exactly where to find the precious seeds they had brought with them from Indiana.

One by one, she laid the little oilcloth-wrapped packages on the table. Each one was marked in Grandma's neat handwriting. PEAS. BEANS. CORN. LETTUCE. CABBAGE. TURNIPS. PUMPKINS. SPINACH.

Father looked over the seeds. "You have forgotten our

most important crop."

Polly was puzzled. "But these are all our seeds."

"I know what's missing," laughed Ben. "You mean the potatoes, Father. We don't need seeds for them."

Polly laughed, too. "All we need is potatoes from the root cellar." (Last week, the whole family had helped to dig a cave where the potatoes would stay cool.)

"First, we must cut the potatoes in little pieces," Mother reminded her.

Father said, "I'll see how much you have planted by the time I come in for lunch." Then he went out to plow. He was always plowing these days. Except when the horses needed a rest, of course.

Yesterday he had plowed and harrowed a patch for their garden. Carefully, Polly placed the seeds in a basket and carried them to the plot. The black soil was full of matted grass roots. Polly tried digging a trench for planting. After a while she said, "I can't make a row, Mother. Why didn't Father plow deeper, so the grass gets covered up better?"

"Think of the horses, Polly," Mother explained. "Plowing this tall prairie grass is hard work for them. The deeper Father plows, the harder it is for the horses."

Ben told Polly, "He isn't plowing very deep in the fields either. That's why we'll plant mostly flax this year. Flax will grow where wheat would not."

"Oh," said Polly. Once again she hacked at the soil with her hoe.

Mother offered, "Let me try. You can do the planting. Drop the peas about two inches apart."

Mother managed to hoe some shallow trenches for the peas and beans and other vegetables. Ben took a turn with the hoe, too.

When all the little seeds had been planted, Ben dropped the hoe and flung himself down on the grass. "Planting potatoes will be even harder. Potatoes need a deeper trench."

"We will take a rest now and get lunch," Mother decided. "In the afternoon we'll plant potatoes."

When Father came in for lunch, he said, "The horses are tired. I'll let them rest for a few hours. Maybe I can help with the garden, if you aren't done yet."

"We still have all the potatoes to plant," Ben said, sounding discouraged. "It's hard, with all those grass roots."

"Then I will do it," said Father. "We'll try using the shovel and just making a hole for each potato."

Planting went faster when Father helped. Polly and Ben walked behind him, dropping the little pieces of potato into the holes he dug. Then they scraped soil into the holes.

When they were finished, Father looked at the sun. It was sinking low in the western sky. "I'll plow for a few hours yet," he decided.

Ben went to hitch up the horses, and Polly followed along to watch. How tired Jasper and Rob looked! Their heads drooped. Their tails drooped. And they were thin. Polly could see their ribs through their dapple-gray coats.

But Jasper and Rob were still willing. When Father said "Giddap" they pulled the plow forward. Plod, plod, plod, went their feet. A thin strip of prairie soil curled away from the plow share.

Ben frowned as he watched the horses plodding down the field. "I hope they don't wear out."

"At least it'll be Sunday again soon," Polly reminded him. "The horses can rest all day Sunday."

"So you think you can walk four miles to Samuel Millers?" Ben asked.

"Of course," Polly said stoutly. "We'd hate to make the horses work on Sundays too, after they've worked all week."

Just then, Polly and Ben heard a shout from Father. "One horse fell down!" Polly gasped.

Ben was already galloping across the furrows. When Polly reached the team, both Father and Ben knelt beside poor Jasper, who lay in a limp heap on the grass. Rob had to struggle to stay on his feet, since he was harnessed to Jasper.

"Come on, Jasper," Father coaxed. "Get up. I know you must feel worn out, but you can't stay here."

Jasper lifted his head, then let it flop down again. After a while Father said, "I guess this team is not meant for so much plowing. Maybe we'll have to sell Jasper and Rob and buy a team of oxen instead."

Ben's face turned pale. Polly wailed, "Oh, no."

Father tried again. "Come on, Jasper. Get up!"

Suddenly they heard a voice saying, "I see you're having a bit of trouble." It was Bill McIlelan, running across the field toward them.

Bill and Father grasped Jasper's harness and tried to

help him to his feet. But Jasper just lay there with a glazed look in his eyes.

Father told Bill, "We may have to sell the team and buy a yoke of oxen."

Bill looked at Ben, then at Polly, then at Father. "You'd be sorry to lose this team, wouldn't you?"

All three of them nodded.

Bill exclaimed, "Well, you certainly can't sell a team if one of the horses is down." Once more they coaxed and pulled. At last Jasper struggled to his feet.

"Listen," said Bill, stroking the trembling horse. "I own a yoke of oxen that's not being used much because I hadn't planned on plowing this spring. I did lots last year. If you're willing to loan me these horses, I'd lend you my oxen."

A smile lit Father's face. "Just what we need for now! Later we'd be glad to have the horses back."

"So, shall we lead the horses to my place now?" Bill suggested. "Another good thing, I have some oats from last year's crop. Your team needs a good feed of oats. Oxen are different. They can go for a long time on a diet of prairie hay."

"All right, Jasper and Rob," said Father. "Here we go to the McIlelans. It's not much farther than home would be."

Polly felt a little bit sad as she followed the dapple-gray team to the neighbors. But at least they were not going far. And they were not being sold.

One of Bill's oxen was red and white, and the other was black and white. "The red one is Roland and the black one is Trim," Bill told them. "They're both quite good-natured—

for oxen, that is."

Father said thank you and drove homeward with the oxen, yoked together by their wooden yoke.

"I wonder why Bill said that," mused Ben. "I wonder why he said they're quite good-natured—for oxen, that is."

"We'll probably find out," replied Father with a wry smile.

Chapter 12

Firewood and Indians

Ben shaded his eyes against the early morning sun. From his perch beside Father on the wagon, he spied a flash of silver beyond the waving prairie grass. "What's that, Father? It must be a lake," he said eagerly.

"Yes, Ben, I think that's Island Lake. Looks like a good spot to go fishing," Father replied.

Ben almost jumped from the seat. "Can we stop now and catch some fish? Mother would be glad for fish."

Father shook his head. "We'll have to come some other time. We must get to the forest as fast as we can if we want to be home before tomorrow night."

Ben settled down again, but he kept his eyes on the

gleaming lake as long as he could. Dreamily he thought how it would be if he and Father and Flip—maybe even Polly—could go fishing some day.

"Whoa!" said Father suddenly. "Do you need a ride?"

At first Ben couldn't figure out to whom Father was speaking. Then he saw a stranger on the other side of the wagon. The man wore a slouchy felt hat pulled far down over his eyes. His beard was a dirty yellow color. His coat and trousers were old and worn.

In answer to Father's question, the man said, "Yes, if you're heading for the forest." Without another word, he clambered over the side of the wagon and sat down beside Father.

"Will you be cutting firewood, too?" Father asked politely as Jasper and Rob started off again.

"I might," the man said shortly.

Father went on. "By the way, I'm Jacob Yoder. Who might you be?"

"Jess Holmes. I'm homesteading west of here." He waved a hand in that direction.

They drove along in silence for a while. The only sounds that broke the stillness were the dull thud, thud of the horses' hooves and the swishing of the wheels in the grass.

"See that mound over there?" Jess said, pointing. "That's an Indian hut."

Ben stared hard. He wanted to say, "Where? I don't see a hut." Then he spied a brown, grassy mound on the left side of the track. A thin plume of smoke spiraled from its peak.

Ben's heart beat fast. Would he see an Indian warrior coming out of this wigwam? A warrior with paint on his face and a bright feather headdress? Might the warrior shoot arrows at them with his bow?

Father said calmly, "I understand the Indians in this area are friendly."

"Right now they are," said Jess. "But it wasn't always so. My parents pioneered in the Dakota Territory back in the 1860's. Those were wild days! Ever hear of the Minnesota massacre?"

"Ah, no." Father glanced uncomfortably toward Ben.

Ben thought he knew what Father was thinking. Father wished Jess wouldn't tell wild Indian stories when Ben was listening.

But there was no stopping Jess. Ben was all ears as he continued, "The Sioux Indians went on a rampage in Minnesota, killing many white settlers. Then the Indians fled to the Dakota territory, and the army came after them. When I was a boy, I watched some battles between Indians and soldiers practically on our doorstep."

"That was quite a while ago," Father said mildly.

"Oh, but there was a battle only four years ago, in 1890," Jess persisted. "It was supposed to be the last battle, but you never know. Some of those Sioux braves escaped to Canada. If they should ever take it into their heads to come back and incite the local Indians to an uprising. . ." He left his sentence hanging.

Ben shivered. By this time even he was wishing Jess Holmes would stop talking about angry Indians.

Jasper and Rob plodded along slowly as the trail

wound upward. Trees grew thick and tall on either side. Father stopped the horses and tied them to a stout tree. Pointing to a huge, fallen tree, he said, "Once we've cut that up, we'll have a load."

Ben wondered if Jess would help them cut up the tree. But he merely said, "Thanks for the ride," and hurried up the trail. Ben and Father set to work with axe and saw.

By noon, Ben was so hungry that he felt he could eat the whole basket of lunch Mother had sent along. Yet he knew it must also last for supper and breakfast and maybe even for tomorrow's noon meal.

All afternoon they toiled. With Father at one end of the crosscut saw and Ben at the other, they pulled it back and forth. Ben was sure he had never worked so hard in his life.

At last darkness fell. Father built a fire and warmed some soup. Ben huddled close to Father, staring at the flames. His eyelids dropped down... down... down.

Father chuckled. "I think we should get our bedrolls."

Ben helped spread the blanket. Then he lay down. It didn't matter that the ground was hard. It didn't matter that he had heard wild Indian stories that day. Ben slept like a log!

The next thing he knew, morning had come and Father was poking the fire to life. For breakfast they fried the eggs that Mother had carefully wrapped in grass to keep them from breaking.

"Ready to work the saw again?" Father asked as Ben chewed down his last bite of bread.

"Yes," Ben answered manfully, though his shoulders

and arms felt sore.

After an hour, they were ready to load the wagon and start for home. Jasper and Rob trotted eagerly downhill. They had not liked being tied up in the forest. They wanted to get home as fast as possible.

"Ben," said Father, several hours later as they neared home. "Let's not tell Polly those stories that Jess Holmes told."

Ben looked up at Father. "Okay," he said.

Chapter 13

Picnic with the Oxen

Water!" yelled Ben, so loudly that Polly and Mother could hear him from inside the house.

Polly had been helping Mother get dinner. When she heard Ben's shout, she ran outside shrieking, "Is it coming? Did you find water?"

There was Ben, all covered with dirt, climbing out of the new well. For days the Yoder family had been well-digging. Ben had done most of it, because Father had to keep plowing. Mother and Polly often helped Ben by cranking the pails of earth out of the well as fast as he filled them.

Beneath the mud on Ben's face was a big smile. "Yes,

there's water down there. Lots of it! I had to hurry to get out of the way."

Polly leaned over to stare into the well. The noonday sun shone right down into it. And yes, there was the glint of water!

"It's a good thing we have a well now," Mother said happily. "The creek has been getting very low with all this dry weather."

Jakie came running to see what all the fuss was about. Just in time, Mother grabbed his trousers. "Careful, don't fall in."

Ben cleaned out the bucket they had been using to crank up the dirt. Then he let the bucket down again. This time when it came up, it was full of cold, fresh, water.

Polly complained, "The water's muddy. We can't drink that."

"In a little while the water will be clear," Mother assured her. "Now I better hurry in to check those potatoes on the stove."

Polly followed her indoors. She set the table and sliced the bread. Then she ran out again to check the sun. It was straight overhead. That meant it was time for Father to come in for the noon meal.

"Why doesn't Father come in?" Polly asked.

Mother kept on stirring the soup. "Maybe he forgot to check the sun. Surely he'll be in soon."

Polly stared across the furrows. Way out there was Father with the oxen. They were so slow, it would take them a while to reach the house.

Then Polly heard something. She said to Mother, "I can

hear Father shouting."

Mother dropped her spoon and came to the door. For a moment she listened. Then a smile spread across her face. "He's shouting at the oxen. I think they don't want to move."

"Oh, are they being stubborn?" asked Polly.

Mother smiled again. "I think so. I know what we will do. Father can't leave the oxen alone out there. That means he can't come in for dinner. So we will take our dinner out to him and have a picnic!"

Polly laughed and went to find Jakie and Ben. Soon they were all on their way across the furrows, each one carrying some food. Even Lisbet clutched a slice of bread in her little hand.

Father mopped his forehead with his big, blue hanky when he saw the family coming. He chuckled. "So you are bringing me my dinner out here, because Roland and Trim won't move."

Mother smoothed out a square in the grass. While she and Polly laid out the food, Father said, "I will get some slough grass for the oxen to eat. Maybe after they have had dinner they will stop being so stubborn."

Polly knew what slough grass was. A slough was a low, marshy spot. The grass that grew there was especially tender.

Once the oxen were munching away, the Yoder family sat down in the grass and asked a blessing on their food. It was May, and the wind blew warm and fragrant across the prairies.

Then Ben remembered to tell Father, "We have a well! I

The children thought a picnic was a great idea!

struck water this morning."

"Ah, that's good," Father said gratefully. "I have to think of that story in the Bible where Jesus met a woman at a well."

Polly begged, "Tell us the story, please."

So Father told how Jesus sat down near a well one day, feeling tired and thirsty. His disciples went to town to buy food. When a Samaritan woman came along, Jesus asked her to draw water from the well for Him.

"How surprised the woman was! You see, Jesus was a Jew. The Jews had very little to do with the Samaritans. In fact, they even looked down on them. To think that a Jewish man would ask a Samaritan woman to draw water for him!

"Then Jesus told her something wonderful and mysterious," Father went on. "He offered to give the woman the living water of everlasting life!

"So now," Father concluded, "when we drink water from our well, we can sometimes remember the blessing of everlasting life that Jesus promised."

The meal was over. The oxen must have been feeling much better. All it took was one word from Father and they were off!

Chapter 14

Firebreak

The warm wind kept blowing and Father kept on plowing and harrowing. Finally, near the end of May, Father said, "It is time to plant the flax."

Ben jumped up happily. "Does that mean we can have Jasper and Rob back, if you've finished plowing?"

Father shook his head. "Sorry, not yet. As soon as the seed is in the ground, I will go on plowing. We want to get even more land ready for next year, you know."

"Oh. So it'll be a while before we have time to go fishing." The disappointment showed in Ben's voice.

"Once the planting is done, we will make time," Father promised cheerfully. "Now, in which packing box will I find our seeds? Do you know, Polly?"

Polly pointed to a box. "We brought the flax seeds in the same box as the garden seeds."

Father opened the seed-bag. He lifted a handful of shiny brown seeds and let them drop down through his fingers.

"What are we going to do with so many acres of flax?" Ben wanted to know.

Father replied, "We will sell the seeds. And we might use some of the stalks to weave linen and make new clothes."

"Polly and I both need a new dress," said Mother. "Father and Ben need new shirts. We could make some linsey-woolsey fabric. We brought spun wool from the sheep we had in Indiana."

"So that's what linsey-woolsey means," chuckled Polly. "Cloth that's made partly from sheep and partly from flax."

Polly went with Father to the field. Father had the flax seeds in a bag at his side. He took some seeds in his hand. Then he swung his arm and let the seeds fly out in a rainbow shape. Over and over he did this, while walking across the black, crumbly soil.

Then Polly noticed something strange. All the way around the edge of the field stretched a plowed strip that was not harrowed. Father did not plant any seeds in that strip.

"Why don't you plant here, Father?" Polly asked.

Father stopped planting and looked at Polly. "That plowed strip is our fire-break."

"What's that?" she wondered.

"Well, sometimes when the prairie is dry there are big fires. Miles and miles of grass get burned up. We wouldn't want such a fire to burn our house, would we?"

"Oh, no," said Polly with a shudder.

"So that's why we leave a bare, plowed strip, to stop a fire if it comes. Fire cannot easily jump across this strip." Father reached into his bag for another handful of seeds. On he moved across the field.

Polly stood stock still. Miles and miles of fire! How terrible that would be, to see the whole prairie on fire.

She ran after Father and asked, "If everything was wet, we wouldn't get a prairie fire, would we?"

"No," said Father. "Rain is just what we need—for two reasons. Rain would discourage prairie fires. And it would help the flax seeds to grow."

"Then we should pray for rain," Polly said earnestly.

"If we do," Father reminded her, "we must also remember to say, 'Thy will be done.' God knows best."

Polly nodded. Then she started back to the house. Suddenly the prairie seemed big and dangerous. She could hardly wait to get back to Mother.

Every night after that, Polly prayed for rain. And one day the blue sky began to fill up with clouds. "I think it's going to rain!" Polly exclaimed.

"That's good," said Mother, peering out the tiny window at the clouds.

Polly ran outside. Rain was beginning to fall. How good the warm, gentle drops felt on her face!

Mother appeared at the door and said, "Better come

inside, Polly. You shouldn't get your woolen dress wet."

But Polly wanted to stay outside. She pointed to the slough, where Father and Ben were cutting grass for hay. "Father isn't coming inside either," she pouted.

"You must come in," said Mother sternly.

Polly obeyed. She stood near the window to watch the rain. Soon it stopped. The sun came out and the clouds scuttled away over the horizon.

"All the clouds are gone," Polly mourned. "We needed more rain than that."

Mother reminded her, "We mustn't complain. God knows best."

There was one good thing about the shower being so little: the hay making didn't have to stop. Before supper, the grass Father had cut last week was ready to bring in. Father and Ben loaded bundles of hay onto the wagon. The oxen pulled the wagon to a spot near the house.

Now it was time to build a haystack. That was fun. As the haystack grew higher, Polly climbed up and slid down the sweet-smelling hay. "Come here, Jakie," she called. "You can do this too."

She helped him climb up the pile. But instead of sliding down, Jakie took a somersault and landed on his face! Polly slid down pell-mell to help the howling boy.

There was blood on his face! Polly began wailing too. "Oh, Jakie, Jakie," she cried, staggering with him to the house.

Mother gathered Jakie into her arms and gently washed his face. "There, there. You have a few scratches. They will get well soon."

Jakie quieted down. Polly sniffled, "I'm sorry, Mother. I didn't take very good care of him."

Mother patted her arm. "Next time it will go better."

Polly's tears stopped as quickly as that morning's little rain shower.

Next morning the flax was up. The fields looked as if someone had taken a brush and washed the black earth with soft green.

"It's like a miracle," Mother breathed to Polly. They stood and watched the rays of the morning sun touching the new, little, green plants.

"The rain helped, didn't it?" asked Polly.

"Oh, yes," said Mother. "To think that so many tiny seeds have sprouted. We must remember to thank God."

Chapter 15

Fire!

Polly's nose twitched. She breathed deeply. She turned this way and that. The smell was everywhere. Smoke! Yet no smoke curled from the chimney. The smell was in the wind.

Trembling, Polly ran to Mother in the garden. "Do you smell it too, Mother? Do you?"

Mother got up from her knees. She sniffed once, twice. Polly watched her face.

Mother gazed toward the west. The horizon was not clear and blue. It was dark and smudged. "Those are not rain clouds," Mother said, and Polly could hear a little tremble in her voice.

"Where is Father?" Polly wondered.

"There." Mother pointed toward the haystack. The oxen lumbered up with a load of hay, and Ben began unloading.

But Father and Ben did not go back to the slough for another load. Instead, Father tied the oxen and hurried over to the garden with Ben right at his heels.

Polly had not often seen Father's face looking like that. His voice sounded strange, too. "There must be a fire," he said. "Coming this way. The wind is from the west. How many buckets do we have, Mother?"

"Two." Her answer came quick and tense. "And the wash tub."

"We want to draw all the water we can," Father said, just as tense, like a spring ready to uncoil. "When the fire goes by, we'll need to watch the haystack. Put out any sparks. We can beat them out with feed sacks."

He turned to Ben. "Right now we'll wet the house roof. Where are the buckets?"

Working fast, as if their life depended on it, Ben and Father drew buckets of water. Splash! They emptied them on the grassy roof. Water dripped down from the ceiling. Polly whimpered to Mother, "I thought this roof is supposed to keep the rain out."

"This is more than just a shower," Mother reminded her. "Father and Ben are pouring whole pailfuls of water on our roof."

"I hope they stop soon," said Polly, watching the drips land on her bed.

"Polly," said Mother. "We are glad if our house can be

saved. If the grass would catch fire, the poles might burn too. Then we wouldn't have a roof anymore."

Polly felt ashamed. To think she was worried about a little water when the whole prairie was on fire!

Jakie could not understand what was going on. He couldn't grasp it when Mother told him that a fire was coming. But he was afraid. So Mother just sat and held Jakie and Lisbet.

Polly didn't really want to go outside—and yet she did. A minute later, she was back inside, clinging to Mother. "I saw it. I saw the fire," she whispered.

Mother opened her arms wider and held her tight, along with Jakie and Lisbet. "Can you be brave, Polly? Can you stay in here with the little ones when the fire comes? I have to help put out sparks."

Slowly, Polly nodded. She wanted to do her part.

Right there, with her arms around the three of them, Mother asked God to keep them safe. Then Polly went to the window. She couldn't help it. She had to see the fire.

"Mother!" she shrieked. "A deer ran right past our window! And there's two more coming across the field, and rabbits, and—"

Mother came to her side. "Those are antelope, Polly. And maybe that animal behind it is a wolf."

"Is the wolf chasing the antelope?" Polly asked in utter bewilderment.

Mother explained, "Those animals are not after each other at all. They only want to escape from the fire."

It was true. Now a coyote scuttled by, and it paid no attention to the other animals, not even the rabbits. The animals did not notice Father and Ben either. They just raced past, tongues hanging out and eyes wild with fear.

Birds, too, fluttered ahead of the smoke cloud. Suddenly a large winged shape plummeted from the sky. The bird had gray wings and a long black neck. It waddled along frantically until it came to the haystack, where it lay down.

"Mother, there's some kind of duck on our haystack," Polly cried.

Mother was putting on her bonnet to go outside. "I will watch out for that duck," she promised. "Now Jakie and Lisbet, you be good while I'm out there. You can watch me fighting sparks with this bag." She smiled as she held up an old feed sack.

Polly wanted to cling to Mother. But instead she smiled bravely and helped Jakie and Lisbet climb onto a chair near the window.

Now the fire had almost reached the firebreak. Would the fire stop? Or would it jump across into the field with the new, little flax plants?

The flames paused, as if they were puzzled. Then they turned and ran both ways along the firebreak. Soon fire was burning all around the Yoder homestead. Even in the sod house, Polly could feel the terrible heat.

And out there in the billowing smoke, three shapes dashed around with their sacks, beating down the sparks. Could they save the garden? Could they save the haystack?

Then the fire was racing away to the east. "I hope the other homesteads have firebreaks, too," Polly said to Jakie in a trembly voice.

"I want Mother," he whimpered. Of course Lisbet began crying, too. No matter how hard she tried, Polly couldn't cheer them up anymore.

At last Mother came inside. Jakie stopped crying in mid-gasp. Mother's face was black! So were her hands and her dress. Lisbet started running to Mother, then she stopped. She didn't know what to make of this black Mother.

"I'm going to wash up," Mother said kindly. "Polly, do you know what? That bird that landed on the haystack is a Canada Goose. One of his wings is burnt. He can't fly anymore."

"Oh, the poor goose," Polly said.

"Maybe his feathers will grow back again," said Mother as she splashed her face. "Polly, can you get more water? Father and Ben will want to wash, too."

Polly stepped outside with the water bucket. The world was a changed place. Ash and cinders lay everywhere. Instead of green grass, there was only blackness beyond the flax fields. The eastern sky still flickered with flames.

But to the west, the sky was now as clear and blue as ever. Not a trace of smoke remained.

Chapter 16

Goodbye, King

The goose stayed. He seemed to consider the Yoder's haystack his new home. Polly planned to make him a pet. She went out to visit him every day. She named him King. He had a kingly way about him, stretching his long neck and turning his head from side to side as he gazed at her.

At first King was not friendly. Polly would sit on the haystack, holding out choice bits of hay. Sometimes she coaxed him in a low voice. But he always waddled sternly away, his injured wing dragging on the ground.

Gradually, King seemed less wary. He would take a few steps toward Polly before strutting away. "I think King is

Polly would coax King with bits of hay.

learning to like me," Polly said excitedly to Ben when he drove up with a load of hay. In spite of the prairie fire, they could still make hay. Parts of the slough had been wet enough that they did not burn.

"Huh. Who wants a wild goose for a friend?" Ben sniffed.

"I do," Polly answered promptly.

"Flip is a better pet any day," Ben declared, stooping to pat the dog's head. Flip bared his teeth and growled at King. King hurried away to the other side of the haystack.

"Bad dog," Polly said severely to Flip. "You mustn't scare King."

Flip wagged his tail as if laughing at her. He was glad the goose had disappeared.

"Why don't you help unload hay instead of playing with a goose, Polly?" asked Ben.

"Oh, sure. I didn't know you want me to help," Polly said quickly.

"Well, Father's busy cutting more grass, so I could use help," Ben replied.

"Are you making two haystacks?" wondered Polly.

"Yes. Father says we might buy a cow after we've sold the flaxseed. So we must make sure there's enough hay for a cow and two horses this winter."

Polly clapped her hands. "A cow! That would be nice. And I hope I can have new shoes. And we need to buy some sugar. I'm tired of doing without sugar."

"We also need a new axe," Ben planned. "And my shoes are too small for me too. . ." As they worked, their pile of wishes grew almost as fast as the haystack.

But all this warm, dry weather, so pleasant for haymaking, was not good for the flax. As day after day passed without rain, huge cracks began to open up in the parched soil. Many flax plants shriveled up.

How hard Mother worked to save the garden! Polly helped too, carrying buckets and buckets of water from the well. But the thirsty soil swallowed up the water without a trace. The cabbages and potatoes and beans threatened to die.

"Why doesn't God send rain?" Polly asked plaintively one evening after Father's bedtime prayer.

"God knows best," Father said. "We must not blame Him for the drought. We knew before we moved out here that the West often has dry years. Apparently this is one of them."

Mother added softly, "Let's not forget that we can still have the blessing of a happy heart, even if our crops don't grow."

"But what will we eat this winter if nothing grows?" Ben wanted to know.

Father looked at him quietly. After a while he said, "I haven't given up hope. We may still get a fair crop."

Because of all the water they carried to it, the Yoder's garden did indeed produce some vegetables. But by late August Father had to admit that the flax crop was a failure. Ben asked unhappily, "Won't we at least bring in the threshing rig to thresh what's there?"

Father shook his head. "Paying the thresher would cost more than what we'd get for the flaxseed."

"You mean the flax is no good at all to us?" Ben asked

bitterly.

Father gave him another of those long looks. "We won't let the flax go to waste. We'll thresh by hand what little seed there is."

"Don't forget," Mother piped up, "we're going to separate fibers from the stalks for spinning and weaving."

So they set to work. After the seeds had been removed, Mother began the long process of extracting fibers. "First the stalks must be 'retted'," she explained to Polly. "See, the outside of each stalk is hard and woody. That must come off. So we will soak the stalks in a tub of water."

Once they had been well-soaked, it was fairly easy to separate the fine fibers from the woody parts. Then came the combing. From the Kanagy family, Mother borrowed a flax comb. It looked like the comb Polly used for her hair, only much larger.

At last Mother had a bundle of fibers ready for spinning. "Maybe it's not enough for all the clothing we would like to make," she said, looking at the small pile of flax fibers. "Oh, well. I don't really need a new dress yet."

Polly said nothing. She knew that her own dresses were getting much too small. What if there were not enough linsey-woolsey for even one dress?

Mother borrowed a spinning wheel from Peter Masts. Jakie, Lisbet and Polly watched in fascination as she set the big wheel to whirling.

"I wish I could learn to do that," Polly said as the spun fiber wound onto the spindle.

"You can," Mother assured her. "I will teach you how."

Just then they heard Flip barking excitedly. Polly and

"I wish I could do that," Polly said.

Jakie scampered out to see what was the matter. There was the dog chasing King, who flapped his wings mightily as he tried to get away.

Suddenly King stopped and turned around. "Hiss-ss!" said the goose, loud and angry. Flip skidded to a stop. King looked twice as big as usual with his feathers fluffed up in rage.

"Yip, yip!" yelped Flip. He turned tail and ran. After him came King, hissing and snapping on his heels.

Polly and Jakie laughed and laughed. But for Flip it was no laughing matter. When King finally stopped chasing him, he slunk back to the house with his tail between his legs.

"So the dog and the goose don't get along anymore," Mother said seriously when Polly and Jakie told her what had happened. "Maybe it's time for King to go away."

"Go away?" Polly repeated in surprise. "But he can't fly."

"Yesterday while I worked in the garden, King was nearby," Mother told her. "I had a good look at his injured wing. Those feathers have grown out beautifully."

"Oh," said Polly. The thought of King going away made her feel sad. King was her friend. Why did she always lose her friends? She had left her Indiana friends far behind. Then Mattie and Kettie, her train friends, had disappeared into the huge prairie. Of course, she had new friends, now. Whenever the families got together on Sundays she played happily with the other girls.

Still, she wished King could stay. Then one morning when she went to fetch water, Polly heard a honking sound overhead. Far, far up in the sky she saw a V of birds, flying southward.

How excited King was! He flapped his wings and honked as loudly as he could. He recognized those voices. They were Canada Geese!

Did the flying geese hear him? Did they turn around and come back? Polly didn't know, but the next day a whole flock of geese had settled in the slough.

And King was gone. All was silent near the haystack. "He must have gone off to the slough," Polly told Mother.

"Let's hope his wing is healed," responded Mother.

Polly thought that over. "I guess King would be sad if he had to stay behind."

For two days, the flock stayed near the slough. Then, on a bright sunny morning, the geese lifted high into the sky and formed a straggling V, heading south.

Polly watched them until they were out of sight. Then she took Jakie and walked across the burnt grass to the slough. The only sound was the wind in the grass. No long, black neck popped up. No kingly head turned to gaze at her with bright eyes.

"Goodbye, King," Polly whispered.

Chapter 17

The Secret

Bill McIlelan had managed to raise some wheat in spite of the drought. He insisted on sharing the wheat with the Yoders. " You need something to make flour with," he said. "Next year you will get a good crop, then you can pay me back."

Carefully the Yoders gathered every poor little vegetable that had survived the summer. They stored the potatoes and turnips in the root cellar. The onions were hung from the ceiling in the house. Father had built a tiny barn, big enough for two horses or two oxen, and there they had stored the pumpkins.

"We may not be able to get enough firewood," Father

admitted. "The dead trees in the Turtle Mountains are free, but we are supposed to pay for any trees we cut down." Though Father didn't say it, Polly knew the rest. You couldn't pay for anything if you didn't have any money.

"So anyway," said Father, looking at Ben and Polly, "we want you to gather all the buffalo chips that you can while the weather is dry. Chips work fine for cooking and heating."

Next morning, even before the frosty nip had left the clear, September air, they set out with baskets to gather chips. At first, it seemed like an adventure to wander across the prairie. Then Polly grew tired of it. Her basket was only half full, yet her legs were weary.

"There's a flickertail burrow," she exclaimed to Ben. "Let's sit here and watch. Maybe a flickertail will pop out."

"Aw, we better keep going," Ben objected.

Polly sat down anyway. "I'm tired. I'm going to rest."

"Well, I'll go on hunting chips," Ben told her. "My basket will be full before yours."

"I don't care," she flung after him. Keeping her eyes on the burrow, she lay back on the ground.

A few minutes later, Ben was back. "Let's go now, Polly! You've rested enough."

"No, I haven't," she snapped. "My legs are still tired."

Ben stood there frowning. At last he said, "We'd better head for home, or else the Indians will find us."

Polly just laughed and stayed in her comfortable spot. "Why do you say that? The Indians are friendly."

Ben shook his head. "You don't know everything I do, Polly. There's reason to be afraid of Indians."

"Really?" Polly sat up and looked at him.

Ben scowled and said, "Actually, it's a secret. I'm not supposed to tell you."

"That's not fair!" wailed Polly. "You've started telling me, now you have to finish."

Ben shrugged. "If I do, you won't like what you hear."

"Tell it," Polly insisted. She didn't like secrets—at least not if she didn't know them.

"Well, you remember the time Father and I went for firewood? We told you about Jess Holmes, the fellow who took a ride in our wagon. But we didn't tell you about his Indian tales. He said the Sioux Indians killed a lot of white people in Minnesota back in the 60's. Then the Indians fled to North Dakota, and the solders came here to fight them. The last battle was only about four years ago."

Polly felt sick inside. She whispered, "Indians and white men killing each other?"

"I said you wouldn't like it if I told you," Ben said. He felt a little sick himself, looking at his sister's pale, scared face. He decided not to tell her the rest of Jess Holmes' tale—that those Sioux braves might come down from Canada anytime and kill more people.

"L-let's go home," Polly quavered.

"We'll go round that way," Ben said, pointing. "We haven't hunted chips along there yet. "

"O-okay," Polly agreed, though what she really wanted to do was go home as fast as her legs would carry her. Though she found a few more chips, her basket was not full when she got home. She was too busy glancing over her shoulder to make sure there were no Indians following them.

"Listen," Ben said sternly when they reached the haystack. "You begged me to tell the secret, so I did. But Father had said I'm not supposed to. So you don't tell them, okay?"

Polly stared at him. She badly needed to talk with Mother about the Indians. But she could see that Ben was in earnest. "All right," she agreed.

"And by the way, Polly," Ben added kindly, "Father doesn't really think there's any danger from the Indians. He thinks Jess was exaggerating."

"O-o-oh," breathed Polly. It certainly helped to know that. Still, Polly could not forget what Ben had said. Whenever she went to get water at the well in the next few days, she hurried back to the house. Playing outdoors was not fun anymore.

Ben noticed that. He felt miserable. If only he had never said anything about the secret!

Not long afterward Father said, "We should go fishing again. It's been a while since we've had a meal of fish."

"Yes, let's," Ben said enthusiastically. He looked at Polly. "You'll go too, won't you?"

Polly hesitated. Then she shook her head. "Guess I'll stay home."

Ben felt sick again. He knew Polly liked fishing. She had greatly enjoyed their first trip to the lake. And Ben also knew why she didn't want to go this time. Later, as he and Father sat together on the shore of the lake, Ben made a decision. Shamefacedly he told Father, "I-I told Polly about Jess Holmes' Indian stories."

Father was quiet. Ben could see the disappointment on his face. Father said sadly, "I had asked you not to."

"I know. I'm sorry. I—well, when Polly caught on that I have a secret, she begged me to tell."

Father looked at him. "I know it's a temptation to try and make excuses. But we must learn not to do that. We must learn to take the blame, fair and square, when we have done wrong. You should not have hinted to her in the first place that you have a secret."

"I'm sorry," Ben said again. "I see that now."

"Mother and I will talk it over before we decide what punishment you should have," Father went on. "And I will have a talk with Polly as soon as I can, to set her mind at rest."

Somehow the fishing was not as exciting as it had been the other time. After catching ten fish, Ben and Father decided they had enough. Ben called Flip, who was sniffing around in the underbrush. Then he shouldered his share of fish and started off.

"Ben," said Father, walking beside him. "I'm glad you confessed your disobedience. Remember, the Bible says, Be sure your sin will find you out."

Chapter 18

Rain at Last

One afternoon at the end of September, a strange team of horses came driving up to the Yoder's home. A man climbed down from the wagon and walked to the door.

"Hello," he said to Mother. "I'm Adam Tracey. My wife Verena and our two boys are on the wagon. We've staked a claim on a homestead west of here." He twisted his hat in his hands. "What we need right now is a place to stay for the night."

"Do stay," Mother said quickly. "Father and Ben could sleep in the barn. We—"

"Let me sleep in the barn," Adam interrupted. "Just as

long as my wife gets a warm bed to lie down, and maybe a bit of warm supper. She hasn't been too well."

"Of course. You may tie your horses near the haystack," said Mother. "My husband will be in for supper soon."

The two little Traceys tumbled from the wagon. Then they stood staring at Polly and Jakie. Polly and Jakie stared back.

Verena did look rather pale and ill. Mother told her to lie down while she and Polly got supper. As soon as Father and Ben came in, everybody squeezed around the makeshift table to eat Mother's good soup and brown bread.

Adam Tracey was a talkative man. He told how he and his family had left Illinois because they could not make a living there. His two brothers already had homesteads in North Dakota. By tomorrow night he hoped to reach their homes. And the Traceys' own homestead was right beside those of his brothers.

After supper, Verena seemed to feel better. She helped with the dishes and talked about their long trip across the prairie in the wagon. "And would you know," she said with a tinkling laugh, "our cat had kittens, right there in the wagon."

"Kittens!" said Polly, forgetting to be shy. "Are they here?"

"Yes. Two are black and white and two are gray," Verena replied. "Maybe you'd like to have a look at them before it gets dark out there."

Out ran Polly. Jakie and the two little Traceys trotted

after her. "There," said the oldest Tracey, pointing to a green box. "In there."

"Oh, the dear things," cried Polly. She cradled one gray kitten against her chest. What a loud purr came from such a tiny creature!

"Would you like to keep two of them?" called Verena from the door.

"Oh, yes," exclaimed Polly. "But we have no cow. Kittens need milk."

"Well, you may keep the mother cat, too," Verena said.

Still clutching the kitten, Polly ran into the house. "Did you hear that, Mother? We could have the cat and two kittens. Think of all the mice they'd catch!"

Mother looked at Polly. "We'll see what Father says."

In the end, the cat stayed. Her name was Rilla and she settled her two remaining kittens in the Yoder's tiny barn. She was a good mother cat and took good care of her kittens.

Polly began to spend all her spare time in the barn. Because of the cats, she wished school would never start. One morning after breakfast she said to Mother, "What if the other children at school aren't nice to us?"

"I don't think you need to worry," Mother assured her. "Don't forget, not all the children will be strangers. Samuel Millers', Jerry Hershbergers' and Peter Masts' children will be there, too."

"Yes, I know," Polly said, though not very happily. After the dishes were washed she went outside. A chilly October wind blew across the brown fields. Overhead, the sky was filling was blue-black clouds. Before Polly reached the barn, a big drop of rain splattered on her forehead.

Polly nestled down in the sweet-smelling hay. Purr, purr said the kittens, climbing around on her apron. Soon the rain on the sod roof grew to a steady drumming. "This is the kind of rain we longed for all summer," Polly said to the kittens.

Then a drop of water hit her hand, another landed on her cheek, and a third wet her forehead. The barn roof was leaking. Faster and faster came the drops, until it seemed to be raining inside the barn.

"I'm going to the house," declared Polly, dumping the kittens from her lap. Rain hit her like a wall as she left the barn. Across the yard she sprinted. Opening the door she gasped, "Mother, it's raining in the—"

But it was raining in the house too, just like it had when Father and Ben poured water on the roof before the fire. Mother was scurrying about, putting pots and bowls under the worst leaks.

At that moment Father came in. He blinked when he saw the dripping ceiling. "It seems we didn't make the roof good enough," he said in a strained voice.

"Well, we tried," Mother said, dragging the tub across the floor.

Father helped her with the tub, then sat down on the only box that had no pot or bowl standing on it. "I'll have to talk with Bill McIlelan again. He should know what to do about a leaking roof."

"The thing is," Ben said unhappily, "it probably doesn't rain like this very often in North Dakota." There was bitterness in his voice. "If only it had rained like this in the summer."

Father rebuked him gently. "Moisture is never wasted on the soil, Ben."

One little bowl was almost full of rain. Polly took it to the door to empty it. "Why, somebody's here!" she said. "A lady is tying her horse out by the barn, and two girls are climbing from the buggy."

"I should help them," Father said, pulling on his soggy coat.

But the three strangers were already at the door. The woman was tall and gray-haired. Mother greeted them, then apologized, "I hope you can excuse our muddy floor. The roof—"

"I know all about leaking roofs," the stranger interrupted. "I'm Elena Whiteside, and these are my daughters, Lora and Patience. The rain feels so good, after all the dry weather, that we don't mind getting wet, do we, girls?"

The two freckle-faced youngsters shook their heads. They smiled at Polly, who smiled back.

Mother offered a packing box for Mrs. Whiteside to sit on. She began speaking about the Mylo school. She told how many boys and girls had been enrolled last term. She explained what textbooks were needed. Then she fixed kindly eyes on Polly and Ben. "You two plan to attend, I assume?"

Mother answered for them, "Yes, they do."

"You'll like the school," Mrs. Whiteside assured them. "The classroom is downstairs, and our living quarters are upstairs. I'm the teacher, you see."

Polly's jaw dropped. This nice, motherly woman was their teacher? Maybe school wouldn't be too bad after all.

Elena smiled. "By this time Lora and Patience have grown used to being taught by their mother." Then a shadow passed across her face. "My husband died two years ago. We were farming, just like you, and living in a sod house."

"Maybe you could tell us how to improve the roof," Father said.

"Build a wooden one, with shingles," Mrs. Whiteside answered. "I guess you know about the Turtle Mountains, where you can buy timber."

Father did not answer. Polly knew why not. There was no money for buying lumber.

Chapter 19

Cold

Polly told no one about her secret hope. No one, that is, except God. "Please God," she prayed on the evening before school started. "Let Kettie and Mattie be at our school. I want so much to see them again."

On the first morning, Father took Polly and Ben to school with the team and wagon. He wanted to be sure they knew the way. The school was a neat, two-story building, looking small and alone on the vast prairie.

Other children were arriving from different directions. Pulling Jasper and Rob to a halt, Father smiled at Polly and Ben. "I hope you have a good first day."

Polly nodded. Something in her throat kept her from

Father took the children to school with the horse and wagon.

speaking. She wanted to linger on the seat beside Father. Instead, she climbed down slowly, clutching her tin lunch bucket.

Seeing the Hershberger boys, Ben hurried over to them. Polly forced her feet to carry her to the school gate. Then someone said good morning, and there was Lizzie Miller with her familiar, wide smile. That made Polly feel better.

How strange it seemed to enter a wooden building again. For Polly it was the first time since leaving Indiana. She liked the clean smell of wooden walls and doors. Inside the classroom were smells of chalk and ink and paper.

Lora and Patience came clattering downstairs. With friendly smiles and hellos they greeted all the girls.

Eagerly, Polly scanned each newcomer's face. But her heart sank after everyone was seated in the desks. Kettie and Mattie were not there. They lived too far away to attend this school.

Polly forgot about her disappointment as the day wore on. Mrs. Whiteside was a very nice teacher, even though she was not at all like Miss Mulligan. She smiled a great deal more than Miss Mulligan ever had.

"I like the Mylo school," Polly said to Mother when she got home that night. "The other children were very friendly. But..."

When Polly didn't say anything more, Mother prompted, "Is something wrong?"

Polly stared down at the dirt floor. "Not really. I—I had hoped Kettie and Mattie would be there."

"Oh," said Mother. "And it turns out they're going to

some other school."

"I prayed," Polly confided. "I asked God to let them be there. But He didn't answer my prayer."

Mother was quick to correct her. "God always answers our prayers—just not always in the way we would like Him to. He knows best. He knows where Kettie and Mattie live, even if we don't. And some day," Mother added, patting Polly's shoulder, "someday I'm quite sure we will find out where Kettie's family lives."

When Ben came in, Mother asked, "Did you stop and chat with Father in the field?"

"Yes. I'm glad he could borrow the oxen for plowing today. The horses needed a break."

"And did you have a good day at school, too?" Mother went on.

"I guess so," he replied. "The lessons were pretty hard. But Mrs. Whiteside is helpful."

Mother said warmly, "I'm glad you both enjoyed your first day at school."

Ben plunked down on a packing box. "But I'll be glad to stay out of school some days to help Father. When is he going for more firewood? He said I could go along when he does."

"That might not be till November," Mother told him. "As long as the ground's not frozen, he wants to keep plowing."

Mother was right. The next trip to Turtle Mountains did not take place till the second week in November. Besides Ben and Father, two other wagons started off early that morning: Jerry Hershberger and John Kanagy, each with one of their boys along.

The three boys were in high spirits, calling to each other as the wagons lumbered along. Though nippy with frost, the air was bright with sunshine. The horses' hooves rang on the frozen track.

As the road led uphill, the horses grew weary. It was mid-afternoon when they finally reached the deepest part of the forest, where fallen trees were still easy to find. Clouds began to cover the sky and a few snowflakes sifted down.

"We'd better fill our wagons before everything gets snowed under," Jerry exclaimed.

Ben looked questioningly at Father. "Does he really think we'll get lots of snow?"

"We might," said Father, throwing the first branch onto the wagon. "Though I've heard they usually don't expect a great deal of snow in this area."

"Not much rain, not much snow," Ben commented.

But that night, the snowflakes covered everything with a thick, white carpet. Starting the campfire was quite a chore. Once the flames leaped high, everyone huddled nearby for warmth.

"Our horses should be blanketed for the night," John said. "I think I'll use the blankets Abe and I had planned to sleep on. We can keep warm if we sit close by the fire, can't we Abe?" he asked his son, who nodded.

Everyone followed John's example. Once the horses were warmly blanketed, the men and boys crowded to the fire. At first, the boys thought it would be fun to stay awake all night. They laughed and talked and made up word games to play. After a while everyone fell silent. The only sounds were the snowflakes hissing in the flames, the crackle of burning branches, and the moaning of the wind, high in the tree-tops.

Ben brushed a layer of snow from his shoulders and lap. He tried to find a more comfortable position. His back felt cold, while his face was uncomfortably warm. His thoughts began to blur, like the whirling snowflakes. Round and round they whirled, hurricanes and tornadoes of snow . . .

Suddenly Ben jerked awake. He'd been sleeping on his father's shoulder. "Sorry," he mumbled.

"Sleep away," Father said. "I can't blame you for being tired. It'll be morning before long."

Finally the dawn-light stole through the trees. They ate quick, cold breakfasts and started for home.

Ben had never felt so cold in his life. The cold reached iron talons beneath his coat. His mittened hands felt like useless lumps. "It must be colder than it ever was in Indiana," he said to Father.

"Maybe it is," Father agreed, keeping his eyes on the steep trail.

Just then they heard shouts up ahead. John's wagon had slipped down a steep bank and overturned. Firewood lay strewn in the snow.

The other two teams stopped and some of the men strained to right the wagon. Ben stayed with Jasper and Rob. He groaned as he watched the men with their shoulders to the upset wagon. Now he'd get even colder because of this delay.

John's wagon slipped down a bank.

Finally they had the wagon upright, and Father hustled toward Ben. Oh good, thought Ben, we'll go now.

But Father had a different idea. "I'll watch the team now, while you help reload the Kanagy's firewood," he said. "That'll give you a chance to get warm. Moving around helps, you know."

Feeling ashamed, Ben climbed stiffly from the wagon. How selfish it would have been not to help John and Abe reload! And Father was right. By the time Ben clambered back on their wagon, he felt warm right to his fingertips.

Chapter 20

A Feeling in the Air

The North Dakota winter was cold. No, the smoke did not freeze before it left the chimney, the way Ben's friend John Mast had said. Nor did Polly have to break the ice on her blanket before she could get up in the morning. But it was still colder than the Yoders had ever experienced. Bill McIlelan said the thermometer in town often showed thirty degrees below zero. Sometimes it showed forty or even fifty below.

There was not much snow, most of the time. But one morning in late January Mother looked out the window and said, "Those clouds make me think of something I heard from Cynthia McIlelan."

Polly peeked past Mother's elbow. The snowy prairie stretched away to the gray sky. Dark, heavy clouds lay along the horizon.

"Cynthia says she can feel it in the air if there's going to be a blizzard," Mother went on. "She says she can even smell it."

Father wrinkled his brow. "Why do you talk of blizzards this morning? We haven't had much snow at all."

"Remember the surprise snowstorm that time you went to the mountains for firewood in November?" Mother reminded him.

"Of course I remember," Father said with a shrug. Then he turned to Polly and Ben. "Are you ready to go to school? I think I'll hitch up Jasper this morning." Bill had loaned them a small, one-horse sleigh that Father used to take the children to school.

Polly asked, "You don't really think we'll get snowed in, Mother, do you?"

"Oh—probably not," Mother answered hesitantly.

"I certainly want to go to school," Polly bubbled. "Today's the spelling match. Mrs. Whiteside divided us into two teams, you know, and each week we have a match. Last week the other team won, but the week before, it was us." Polly and Ben grinned at each other, remembering the fun.

"So you two are on the same team," remarked Father as he put on his overcoat. "It's nice that you don't have to compete against each other."

Mother tucked the last sandwich in Polly's lunch bucket. "Remember, if there ever is a blizzard and we can't come to get you, then just stay with Mrs. Whiteside for the night."

"Oh, Mother," said Ben as he went out the door, "why do you keep talking about blizzards?"

Jasper started off at a fast trot. He knew exactly where the Mylo school was. Soon Ben and Polly waved goodbye as they got out of the sleigh at school.

The spelling match began right after noon. Outdoors, the wind was rising, but nobody paid any attention. Mrs. Whiteside allowed the children to push aside the desks. Then she arranged the pupils along the north and south walls of the classroom. The youngest ones of each team were near the front.

"CAT," she began, looking at Toby Mettler, the tiniest boy. Confidently he spelled the word back to her.

"BAT," said the teacher, turning to the youngest team member on the other side. As she went down the line, the words got harder. Polly jiggled nervously from one foot to the other when her turn neared.

"TRAVEL," said Mrs. Whiteside.

Before Polly could spell it, Hal Jennings pointed to the window and exclaimed, "Look at that!"

Every head turned. Polly gasped. Snow whirled so thickly past the window that the panes seemed covered with wool.

"Blizzard!" cried Rick McPhee. Suddenly, all the children were talking. The spelling bee was forgotten.

Mrs. Whiteside rapped a ruler on her desk to stop the buzz of voices. "Children. You know our plan for a storm. Start home right away if the blizzard is not too bad and if you have your own horse. If you don't, wait for your parents to fetch you. And if they don't come, stay right here."

Just then a knock sounded on the door, and there was Roger McPhee, looking like a snowman. "Rick—Sue—Millie—get your coats and we'll be off."

In less than fifteen minutes, 28 of the pupils had disappeared into the swirling snow. Only Polly and Ben were left. Lora and Patience led Polly upstairs, gleefully making plans for a night together.

Minutes later, Mrs. Whiteside called up the stairs, "Your father is here to get you, Polly."

Polly hurried down. Father's coat was all snowy. But where was his hat?

"The wind got my hat," Father said ruefully. "I've never seen a storm like this."

Mrs. Whiteside said soberly, "Shouldn't you stay? You're new to the area, and not used to blizzards. Things may be better in the morning."

Father shook his head. "My wife is expecting me. Are you ready, Polly and Ben? Tie your scarves around your face, like this."

Mrs. Whiteside declared, "You must not go bareheaded, Mr. Yoder. Wait, I'll get something for you upstairs." Moments later she returned with a stocking cap.

"Thanks," said Father, pulling the cap over his hair.

He looked so strange that Polly wanted to laugh. But she didn't. Things were too serious. Going outside was like walking into a wall of snow. Where had Father tied Jasper? The horse was nowhere in sight.

Father peered into the whiteness. "Over there," he said. Polly put up her arm to shield her face and followed him blindly.

Sure enough, there was Jasper, his dapple-gray coat all white with snow. Father untied him and they were off. Thump! The sleigh struck something and toppled on its side. The three of them spilled onto the snow.

"That's spill number seven," chuckled Ben. Upsets in this little sleigh were so common that the children were keeping track, just for fun. Righting the sleigh, they moved blindly on, into the howling wind. Soon they had spill number eight. By spill number nine no one was laughing anymore.

"It's the wind," Father said. "The sleigh simply gets pushed over."

"Are we going to make it?" whimpered Polly. Already she felt cold to the bone.

Holding the reins, Father stood beside the sleigh. "I think I will take you back to school. Mrs. Whiteside will gladly keep you for the night."

"What about you?" Ben asked.

"I'm going home. Mother would be worried if I stayed," Father said firmly.

"Where's the schoolhouse?" Polly asked in bewilderment.

"We can follow our tracks back. We haven't come far, with all those upsets." Father took them right to the schoolhouse door.

"How will you ever get home, Father?" Polly fretted.

"Don't worry about me," Father replied, pulling the

stocking cap down farther. "Trust in God." And with that, he turned Jasper into the driving snow.

Chapter 21

Long Night

Father could not understand why Jasper was so stubborn. He simply did not want to go in the direction Father thought he should. Was it because Jasper didn't like heading into the wind?

Time seemed to stop for Father, there in the swirling whiteness. How far had he come? And how many times had the sleigh flipped over? Finally, Father decided to leave the sleigh behind. With half-frozen fingers he unhitched Jasper and climbed on his back.

More time passed. Were they going around in circles? Suddenly Father felt Jasper stumble. He heard the clang of hooves on steel.

"The railroad!" he exclaimed. Now he would not get lost. Not if he followed the track.

But which way was Mylo? And which way was Rollo? Father simply did not know.

He would have to make up his mind, and follow the track in one direction or the other. Either way, he would probably arrive at a warm place. But Mother would not know where he was.

Then Father realized that he couldn't follow the track on Jasper's back. He would have to get down on his hands and knees and feel for the iron rail.

"Sorry, Jasper," he said as he slid off the horse's back. "I hope I see you again."

So Father left the horse standing in the flying snow. Getting down on his hands and knees, he began to crawl towards safety.

Meanwhile, back home, Jakie was full of questions. "Why doesn't Father come? Why don't Ben and Polly come?" he asked Mother, over and over again.

"Maybe the sleigh dumped," she told him. "That would mean it's taking them longer."

Slowly the swirling whiteness turned to howling darkness. Mother's answers to Jakie's questions changed now. "Do you know what? I think they decided to stay at school. They would all have room to sleep there."

Jakie began to cry. "I wish they would come home."

"Let's eat supper," said Mother. They had been waiting to eat, hoping the others would come.

Lisbet ate happily. She was too young to understand how serious the storm was. Jakie ate a little bit of soup, but he didn't seem hungry. Neither was Mother.

Soon afterwards, she put Lisbet to sleep. Jakie didn't want to sleep. Mother sat holding him until his head began to nod. Finally he could not stay awake any longer.

Mother did not sleep. There was only one thing for her to do. All through that long, long night she prayed as she kept the fire going.

Morning came. The storm's fury died down. Through the part of the window that was not covered with snow, Mother could see the shape of the barn. At last the wind stopped. How quiet it seemed!

Jakie's head popped out from under the blanket. "Is Father home?"

"Not yet," Mother said unsteadily.

Carefully she opened the door. Snow fell inside. The shovel stood right there, so she began shoveling.

Now the sun's first rays slanted across the dazzling snow. Mother shaded her eyes to see better. What was that beside the barn? Why, if was Jasper. He raised his head and whinnied. The sleigh was nowhere to be seen.

Mother felt sick. She hoped Jakie would not notice Jasper right away. She needed time to think before he started to ask questions.

Then Mother saw something else. In the distance were three figures, wading through the snow. She watched them draw nearer. The sick feeling went away and happiness took its place.

"Jakie," she called. "Father and Polly and Ben are walking home."

Jakie stared at Mother. Her voice had never sounded

like that before. Then he jumped up and shouted, "Are they really coming?"

Mother hugged him tightly. "Yes, Jakie, they are. Father looks funny. I don't know where his hat is. It seems he has a stocking on his head."

That was the first question Jakie asked when Father struggled through the snow to the door: "What's that on your head, Father?"

Of course, Mother had many other questions. But they could wait until she had helped Polly and Ben out of their stiff, frozen coats. They could wait until she hugged them and made sure no one had frozen fingers or toes. Then at last she said, "You must have stayed at school for the night. But why did Jasper come home?"

"You mean he's here?" exclaimed Father.

"Right out there by the barn, on the side away from the wind," replied Mother.

Father shook his head slowly. "So if I had given him his head, Jasper would have brought me home." Then he let out a sigh of relief. "I'm so glad he's all right. I didn't know if he'd make it, when I abandoned him." And he began to tell about the hard decision he'd faced, there on the railroad track.

Mother clutched his arm. "So you didn't stay at school."

"No. I suppose I should have. I was so worried about you . . ." Father's voice broke. "Anyway, I reached the hotel in Mylo. They brushed me off and warmed me up. The minute the storm died down, I headed for the school. Polly and Ben were surprised to see me come walking in."

Polly nodded. "But we sure were glad. Mother, that seemed like a long night."

"Yes," said Mother. "Yes, it surely did."

"But God was with us all," said Father. "Let's thank Him for His loving care."

Chapter 22

Promised Blessings

Polly liked to watch Mother sewing her new linsey-woolsey dress. How fast her needle flashed in and out of the rough, brown fabric!

Weaving the fabric on the Kanagy's loom had taken a long time. Winter was nearly past when Mother began sewing the dress. Now at last, it was nearly finished.

Mother's needle stopped. She made a knot in the thread. "Polly, please go and get some potatoes. It's time to make supper."

Polly took the tin bowl and stepped outside. The sun was shining brightly. April had arrived and spring was here. New green grass was growing in the fields.

Lifting the heavy sod trapdoor, Polly climbed down the little ladder. Only a few rays of sunshine managed to slip in to help Polly find the potatoes. She could hardly believe her eyes. There were only a few potatoes left! With her hands, she felt around on the cold, damp floor. It was true. Only one little pile of potatoes remained.

Polly filled the bowl and climbed out. Carefully closing the trapdoor, she hurried inside. "Mother, what are we going to do? The potatoes are nearly used up. It will be months before we have new ones in our garden."

Mother kept on sewing. "I guess we will just have to do without potatoes for a while."

"But what will we eat? We've had no turnips either, since February," Polly fretted.

"We still have plenty of wheat from the McIlelans, Polly. Father says we needn't go hungry as long as he can shoot antelope and rabbits. And then there's the fish he and Ben catch in the lake."

"Well, yes," Polly said slowly. She knew Mother could make good soup with antelope and rabbits. But Polly liked potatoes.

"God's goodness is never-failing," Mother stated, her needle as busy as ever.

Polly offered, "Shall I peel the potatoes for supper? Then maybe you can get my dress finished in time for tomorrow."

It was a special Sunday—and not just because of Polly's new brown dress. Preacher Henry had come on the train from Indiana! Since Samuel Millers had the biggest house, the families all gathered there.

Polly sighed happily as she sat on a little stool in the corner beside Lizzie Miller. How familiar it seemed to hear Henry preaching again, and to see his eyes glowing like black coals. He talked of many things. He told about the world's first rainbow that God put into the clouds after Noah left the ark. "The rainbow is a sign of God's promised blessings," said Henry. "If we obey Him, those blessings are as sure today as they ever were."

And then Henry quoted the verse Polly had heard him repeating many, many times. The way he said it in a powerful, ringing voice, you knew it was important and it was true: "'Jesus Christ, the same yesterday, and today, and forever.'"

That Monday, Mrs. Whiteside had a surprise for her pupils. "We need practice in letter-writing and penmanship," she announced. "So I wrote to the teacher of the Umbleton school and asked her to send me a list of her pupils' names. We are going to do a letter exchange!"

Mrs. Whiteside paused and looked at the children. Polly waited eagerly. This sounded like an interesting project.

"On the chalkboard I have a list of the Umbleton pupils' names." Mrs. Whiteside snapped up a map of the world that had been covering the list. "I will help you choose a partner who is your own age. Then you will write a letter to him or her. Later, they will write back."

Polly began to scan the list of names. Suddenly her heart beat faster. Keturah Magidoff! Matilda Madigoff!

At last, almost a year after losing them, she had found her friends. Now she knew the name of their school. And she could write to them!

Timidly she put up her hand. "Please, may I write to Keturah or Matilda?" she asked.

Mrs. Whiteside looked questioningly at her. "Why yes, you may. Do you know them?"

"I met them on the train when we moved here," Polly replied. She could easily picture both girls in her mind. Kettie with her brown hair and Mattie with her yellow hair. And she still remembered the soft feel of the little pink, homemade ball that had been the beginning of their friendship.

How eagerly Polly began writing that letter to Keturah! Of course, she had to take her time, and practice her best penmanship. But there was so much to write that she was afraid it wouldn't all fit onto the sheet the teacher had given her.

"I can hardly believe that I've found Kettie and Mattie," Polly bubbled to Ben as they walked home from school. "Think of it. For a whole year I didn't know where they were."

Ben shrugged. He wasn't sure why Polly was making such a fuss about those two girls. He pointed and said, "Look! Father has started plowing."

Polly turned her head. There was Father with Bill's oxen, one red and one black. Steadily the furrow fell away from the plowshare. "That means spring is really here," Polly said. "Soon we can plant the garden. Maybe this year we'll get lots of rain, then the vegetables will grow well."

Ben nodded. "And maybe this year we'll have a good crop of wheat. We'll make lots of money, and—"

"We'll buy a cow, and new shoes, and sugar, and fabric for Mother's dress," Polly cut in.

"And a new axe, and lumber to make a nice table and chairs," Ben went on. "Maybe we'll even have enough money to build a real house!"

Polly clasped her hands together. "Oh, I just have a feeling that things will be different this year."

Ben couldn't wait to talk with Father, so he went right out to the field, while Polly hurried to the house. Mother greeted her with a smile. "You're home in good time. Do you know what? There's something on the roof that you should see. Father found it when he went up to make a few repairs."

"I'll go up right now," exclaimed Polly. It wasn't hard to reach the roof of their low, sod house. All she had to do was drag a box and climb up.

What a pretty sight met her eyes. Beautiful little pink flowers were blooming among the new green grass on the roof. Polly picked a handful of the blossoms and carried them down. "Aren't they nice?" she said to Mother.

"Yes, they are," said Mother. "And remember how disappointed you were that we can't have a wooden roof? Well, such pretty flowers wouldn't grow on shingles."

"I'm glad we have a sod house with a grass roof," Polly declared. "Imagine—blossoms on the roof! It sounds like a poem."

"These flowers are like the rainbow, the sign of God's promised blessings," said Mother.

Polly buried her nose in the sweet-smelling petals. "Ben and I were talking about all the things that might

Beautiful pink flowers were blooming on the roof.

happen this year. We might get a good wheat crop, and lots of money to buy a cow, and lumber, and—"

"We don't know what God's plan is for that kind of blessings," Mother interrupted. "But this we know: God loves us, and He sent His Son to show His love. Whether or not we have plenty of money, we can have happy hearts if we obey God."